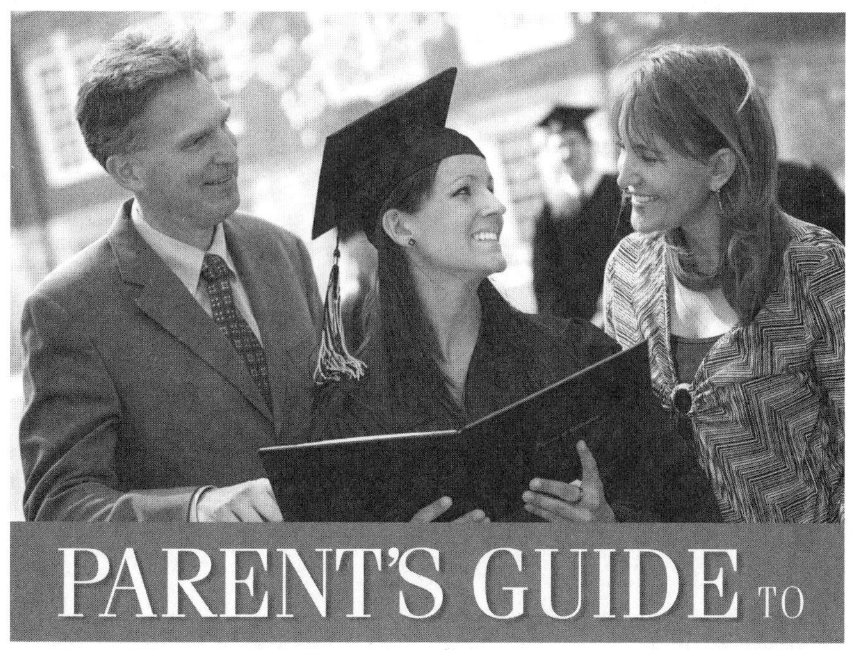

PARENT'S GUIDE TO College and Careers

HOW TO HELP, NOT HOVER

BARBARA COOKE, M.A.

Parent's Guide to College and Careers: How to Help, Not Hover

Published by JIST Works, an imprint of JIST Publishing
7321 Shadeland Station, Suite 200
Indianapolis, IN 46256-3923

Phone: 800-648-JIST Fax: 877-454-7839
E-mail: info@jist.com Web site: www.jist.com

Acquisitions Editor: Susan Pines
Development Editor: Stephanie Koutek
Cover and Interior Designer: Aleata Halbig
Cover Illustration: Sean Locke, iStockphoto
Interior Layout: Aleata Halbig
Proofreaders: Paula Lowell, Jeanne Clark
Indexer: Cheryl Lenser

15 14 13 12 11 10 9 8 7 6 5 4 3 2

Library of Congress Cataloging-in-Publication Data
Cooke, Barbara, 1951-
Parent's guide to college and careers : how to help, not hover / by Barbara Cooke.
p. cm.
Includes index.
ISBN 978-1-59357-785-8 (alk. paper)
1. College majors. 2. Vocational guidance--United States. 3. Occupations--United States. 4. College choice--United States. I. Title.
L901.C838 2010
378.1'98--dc22
2010009522

ISBN 978-1-59357-785-8

For Matt and Chris

Who consistently frustrated my every attempt to be a helicopter mom

Acknowledgements

I would like to thank my husband, Sid Cooke, and my friend Debra Box for their unfailing support and encouragement at each stage of this project.

I would like to thank my wonderful team members in the Advising and Counseling Center at MCC-Maple Woods, whose years of experience, both as college personnel and parents, added so much to this book.

I would like to thank my many other friends and colleagues, especially Ann Schwartz, Robin Stimac, Dawn Hatterman, Shelli Allen, Colleen Brown, and Kate Duffy, for their ideas, enthusiasm, and support. I would also like to acknowledge the many great career-planning and educational professionals I have worked with over the years, including Caryl Neinas, Janice Benjamin, Kitty Wilson, Lorrie Eigles, and Marsha Dufner, all of whom helped me grow and develop as a career counselor.

Finally, I would like to thank my sons, Matt and Chris Pryor, and my daughter-in-law, Christine, for their honesty, insight, and humor in developing the ideas presented in this book.

Contents

Introduction

If you are the parent of a college student, you're getting a bad rap. You're suspected of being a helicopter parent before you ever walk through the college doors.

The term "helicopter parent" has been used in recent years to describe adults who pay extremely close attention to their children, particularly at educational institutions. You've heard the horror stories. There's the mom who decorates her son's dorm room with Ralph Lauren sheets. There's the dad who e-mails his daughter's professor to argue about a grade. There's the parent who insinuates himself into the job search, sitting in the waiting room while Junior interviews for a job and hounding human resources to negotiate a better deal.

The rise of helicopter parenting has a number of causes. Educators tend to focus on the sociological ones. They point to smaller family size, parental over-protectiveness in the wake of Columbine and 9/11, and technological advances such as cell phones and e-mail that give parents instant access to their children at all hours of the day and night.

Parents tend to focus on the economic reasons. They point to the skyrocketing cost of a college education, the potential burden of student-loan debt on their children and themselves, and the uncertain job market their children will face, particularly in times of economic change.

Chances are you don't want to be labeled a helicopter parent. You understand the long-term problems your child will face if you micromanage your child's young adulthood. At the same time, given what you are paying for college and the uncertain job market your child will face, you want to be involved. How can you do this in a constructive way?

The fact is helicopters do more than hover, swoop, and land. Helicopters are extremely versatile flying machines. Their design allows them to see the big picture and identify potential trouble spots before people on the ground experience major accidents. Their flexibility allows them to stop in mid-flight, turn around, and fly in another direction. This is the kind of positive helicopter coverage more young people need.

As a parent, I understand the balancing act of knowing when to help and when to hover. I know what it is like to deal with the bureaucracy of both public and private institutions. I have experienced the frustration of not knowing how my child was doing because I couldn't see his grades. I have run the numbers and evaluated financial aid. I know what it is like to try to persuade a student to stay in college when he questions, "What's the point?"

As an educator, I know the curves and crash points that can derail the college journey. I routinely work with students who have $20,000 in student loans and only 40 college credit hours to show for it. I regularly see students borrowing for remedial courses to learn academic material they could have learned in high school. I watch economically disadvantaged students use student loan money to pay for housing, child care, and transportation, only to quit college because they were trying to manage too many obligations at once. I watch economically advantaged young people use student loans to maintain their lifestyle, only to find themselves out of college and deep in debt. Mistakes made in college can be very costly.

For these reasons, I believe that you, as a parent, need to get involved in your child's career planning. There are constructive and destructive ways you can do this. I have written this book to give you the constructive ways. I have outlined some simple interventions that are easy to use and easy to understand.

The bottom line is that at the end of whatever level of education your child achieves, he or she will enter the job market. At that time, your child will need to have skills employers want and a network of contacts to get ahead. You, as a parent, are one of the main career resources for your child. You are one of your child's best career coaches and mentors. This book will give you the career-planning tools you need to pilot your parent helicopter in a helpful rather than hovering way.

CHAPTER 1

Preparing for College—and Beyond!

Imagine that your best friend wants to borrow money. She asks for $80,000 to go into business for herself.

You take a deep breath and consider your friend's request.

Eighty thousand dollars is a lot of money. You have some of it in savings, but you would have to borrow the rest. Your own job situation is unstable due to downsizings and corporate mergers, and you realize you haven't saved enough to retire. Because of these factors, you are hesitant to take on more debt at this time.

You love your friend very much. You want to help her in any way you can. You decide to ask your friend for more details before you write the check.

You friend enthusiastically explains that she wants to relocate to a city 500 miles away. This city is conveniently located one hour from the mountains, which will enable her to ski and hike on weekends. Your friend has several friends who already live in this community, and all of them say it is the perfect place to live. Your friend isn't sure what she wants her business to be—something working with people or animals, or maybe something in theater. She isn't going to worry about this now. There will be plenty of time to decide what she wants to do after she relocates. She promises to keep you posted on the progress of her venture, but reminds you that it is her life and her decision. She would consider it overly controlling for you to put restrictions on the funds.

Would you lend your friend the money?

Chances are you would want more of a game plan before signing the check. You would want to know more about your friend's goals, the strengths she brings to the venture she proposes, and some assurance that your money will be used wisely. You would want to know that your friend had done her homework and could show some proof that she was adequately prepared to establish and succeed in the business she would ultimately choose. You wouldn't hand over $80,000 to anybody without a mutual understanding of how the money would be spent and some assurance that the outcome would be positive. This is common sense.

But common sense is often not part of the planning for one of the biggest investments most American families will make—the investment in a college education for a child. In the swirl of emotion and sophisticated marketing tactics that surround college recruitment in the United States today, many parents abandon their own common sense when it comes to helping their children with college and career decisions.

Are You a Helicopter Parent?

Consider this real-life scenario:

Ashley is completing her freshman year at Neighboring State U. On the phone recently, Ashley told her mom that she was changing her major from political science to athletic training. She explained that she met someone at a party who had just gotten a cool job with a baseball farm club near Neighboring State U.

Ashley was a strong student in high school, involved in a variety of activities. She was well liked by her peers and a good worker at her part-time job as a sales clerk at a clothing store in the mall. She attended a large suburban high school that was academically rigorous, at least for good students like Ashley.

Ashley chose political science as a major because she had heard that was the best preparation for law school. Her stated career goal was to become a lawyer, something she had talked about from middle school on.

Ashley went off to college with 15 hours of college credit, or the equivalent of one full semester of college work. She was aggressively recruited by a number of colleges and universities. At the recommendation of her high school counselor, she applied to six schools. A major factor in her decision was which institution would give her the best deal when it came to financial aid. Ashley was attending Neighboring State U on a financial-aid package of scholarships, grants, and student loans, which her parents, Kathy and Bob, planned to repay themselves. They didn't want Ashley to start her adult work life burdened with student-loan debt.

Kathy, Ashley's mom, had attended college for two years and dropped out of college to go to work. She was now a successful insurance professional who had been out of work three times in the last 15 years because of corporate reorganization and downsizing. She had always been able to find another job and enjoyed her current job.

Bob, Ashley's father, had a bachelor's degree and 20 years of experience as an IT professional. After 9/11, he was laid off when his job was offshored to India. It took him 18 months to find another job with comparable pay. The time of Bob's unemployment was stressful for the whole family.

When Ashley told Kathy about her proposed major change, Kathy's first reaction was to erupt and say, "How are you going to support yourself with an athletic training degree?" But she restrained herself and told Ashley she would support her in any career choice she made, but she wanted Ashley to do some research and tell her what job prospects she would have with an athletic training major.

A week later, Ashley called Kathy to report in. She said she'd talked with her freshman advisor and the advisor in the athletic training department. She had also talked to some friends who were athletic training majors themselves. Ashley told Kathy she would be able to make $50,000 a year, easy, as an athletic trainer. She would, however, have to get a master's degree in order to make the big bucks.

Kathy related this conversation to Bob, who did erupt and wanted to call Ashley immediately and demand to talk to her advisor at Neighboring State U. Kathy reminded Bob that he was barred by federal privacy laws from getting any information about Ashley from college personnel. Bob e-mailed Ashley and said he wanted to talk to Ashley and her academic advisor. Ashley replied that she didn't want Bob talking to her advisor. She said that changing majors was a normal part of college life and that most college students changed majors at least three times. Ashley told Bob it was her life and she knew what she was doing. She said Bob and Kathy needed to "let go of it" and allow her to make her own decisions.

Are Bob and Kathy overly controlling "helicopter parents," attached to their daughter by the world's longest umbilical cord, the cell phone? Are they meddling in Ashley's freedom of occupational choice?

Or are Bob and Kathy worried parents who have a legitimate fear that a huge investment of time and money is in danger of being squandered?

The problem is that none of the well-meaning adults in Ashley's life—her parents, high school teachers, or counselors—had ever asked Ashley to develop career maturity. Their sole focus had been developing Ashley's academic maturity. Their goal since elementary school had been getting Ashley into college and making sure she was academically prepared to succeed at college-level coursework. At Ashley's high school graduation, all the adults in her life congratulated themselves. They had achieved their goal. Career maturity would happen later. If Ashley just got into the "right" college, she would "find herself" and everything would fall in place.

But now things were not falling into place. If anything, they seemed to be unraveling. Bob and Kathy explained to Ashley that they had nothing against athletic training as a career, but they were worried that Ashley had not considered all her options. They were concerned that Ashley was not being realistic about the job market she would face, and they were worried about the cost of Ashley's education. Bob and Kathy were paying $15,000 per year for Ashley to attend Neighboring State U. This was over and above the amount Ashley was contributing through scholarships. Each additional semester Ashley spent in college deciding what she wanted to do would cost Bob and Kathy $7,500. These factors made them very eager to help Ashley get from point A, going to college, to point B, leaving college and starting a satisfying first career.

Thirty years ago, when Bob and Kathy were in school, this situation would not have been a problem. Ashley could have graduated from college with any major and landed on her feet in the job market. In the 1970s, going to college without a clear goal or understanding of the job market was an acceptable career-planning strategy. No matter what degree you earned or what you majored in, you could have graduated from college and eventually found a college-level job. Your main fear would have been getting "trapped" in a job you didn't like until you retired at age 65.

All of that has changed. Young adults like Ashley face a very different job market from the one you entered 30 years ago. Management ranks that absorbed liberal arts graduates have been flattened. Large government social service agencies that provided good jobs to your baby-boomer friends have seen their funding slashed. Many routine clerical jobs have been computerized or shipped overseas, and more complex jobs requiring higher education are now being outsourced to other countries as well.

It will take more than a college degree for your child to be successful in today's economy. Your child will enter a work environment that has been structurally reshaped, on both a national and international level, in the course of her lifetime. And the competition for jobs in this "New Economy" is going to be intense.

What Is the "New Economy"?

The "New Economy" is a term used to describe the U.S. economy since the early 1980s. The New Economy is characterized by advances in technology, changes in government policies, and increased global competition. It is contrasted with the "Old Economy" that greeted college students like Bob and Kathy in the 1970s.

The New Economy has seen the deregulation of entire industries, such as trucking and airlines, resulting in intense competition among the companies that survived. Routine, repetitive jobs that can be performed by technology have been eliminated, and tasks that can be digitized and transmitted over the Internet have been offshored. Cost cutting, hiring freezes, and capacity-management strategies have increased U.S. productivity to all time highs. Businesses are reluctant to hire additional full-time, permanent employees because of the high cost of health-care benefits. Temporary, contract, and contingent workers are often hired to complete projects on an "as needed" basis. Tax cuts have resulted in fewer jobs in education, social services, and government contracts. All of this has dramatically changed the job market your child will enter.

Some of the changes in the New Economy look like this:

Old Economy	New Economy
Manufacturing industries	Service industries
Job titles	Skill sets
Job security	Employability
U.S. economy	Global economy
Seniority	Job performance
Assembly line	Project team

Here are some key points to be aware of:

- The United States has moved from an economy built on manufacturing tangible goods, such as steel, textiles, and washing machines, to an economy built on providing services, such as financial, health-care, and software design services. Jobs moved with these changes.
- Job titles are no longer stable. New skill sets are constantly being added to old job titles, creating new jobs like "nuclear medicine technologist" and "network security manager." Almost every job in every industry has been changed in some way by technology.
- There is little or no job security anymore. The Old Economy expectation of being able to find a secure job with one company that would last until you retired at 65 is simply unrealistic. Instead, there is "employability," which means having marketable skills that businesses want and carrying those skills from job to job as the demands of the labor market change. It means being able to communicate your skills on a regular basis in job interviews and on resumes.
- Global competition has resulted in many jobs—both blue-collar production jobs and white-collar service jobs—being moved overseas.
- Old Economy companies that promoted on seniority are few and far between. Job performance is the criterion for advancement in most companies today.
- Assembly-line jobs have been automated or shipped overseas to control labor costs. The jobs remaining in the United States are much more likely to be completed by flexible work teams composed of people with a variety of skill sets who must communicate effectively to get the job done.

Given all these changes, what are some common-sense things that you can do to help your child land on her feet in this kind of job market? What are some actions you can take to ensure your college investment pays off in the way both you and your child hope?

CHAPTER 2

Partnering for Success

There are many constructive, developmentally appropriate things you can do to help your child with career planning. But first, you probably need to overcome your own ambivalence about getting involved at all.

Getting Involved in Your Child's Career Planning

If you are a boomer or post-boomer-era parent, you probably have some reservations about playing a part in your child's career decision making. You believe in freedom of occupational choice. You reject a European-style system of education in which young people take a test at age 16 to determine whether they will go to university or into vocational training.

Because of this, you don't place much emphasis on career planning in high school. You believe that should happen later, when your child is in college. You don't want anyone—yourself or others—to pressure advanced students into premature decision making. You don't want anyone to suggest that students with lower academic skills settle for less than a four-year degree. You question whether any eighteen-year-old can make an informed career choice, as many of the jobs he will hold have yet to be created. You believe that all young people should have the chance for higher education and all young people, especially your child, deserve a second chance. And you are willing to commit your tax dollars, as well as your personal savings, to fund these efforts.

At the same time, you are worried about money.

One year at a four-year private college now costs approximately $40,000 in tuition, fees, room and board and books. One year at a state's main, flagship public institution now costs approximately $20,000.

This means that you, as a parent, are looking at a $160,000 investment in private education or an $80,000 investment in public education for your child to earn a four-year bachelor's degree. This is provided your child can finish a degree in just four years. You are aware that the cost of college has exceeded the rate of inflation for the past 20 years, and you believe college costs will continue to increase. You know that students cobble together financial-aid packages to reduce the sticker price of college, but you also know that students and their families are borrowing money at increasingly high interest rates to pay for a college degree.

Because of all this, you feel torn. You want your child to be free to make his own choices, but you know poor choices are expensive. You are eager for your child to go to college, but you also want your child to finish in a timely manner. Your long-term economic goal is for your child to become an independent adult who has a good job and is self-supporting. But how is this supposed to happen? If you, as a parent, should keep your hands off when it comes to guiding your child's career choice, how is that career choice to be made?

Your answer, if you are like most boomer-era parents, is "by going to college." You believe that college is the place your child will find himself. If you just get your child into the right college, everything, including a good job, will all work out.

If the economy today worked the way it did when you were in school, this would be a reasonable expectation. Thirty or forty years ago, anyone could roll out of college with any major and expect to land a good job with benefits. The U.S. economy was structured to absorb unfocused college graduates. Management ranks were expanding. Companies were willing to bring young people into organizational hierarchies, train them to accomplish organizational goals, and move them up the corporate ladder. These companies offered stable jobs with good benefit packages.

Consider Jeff's experience.

Jeff graduated from State U with good grades and a bachelor's degree in history in 1975. His work experience included editing the sports section of the student newspaper, managing a public swimming pool, and working as an orderly at a hospital during the academic year.

At the beginning of his senior year in college, Jeff went to the career placement center on campus. This was the office where seniors went to find jobs. He signed up for eight on-campus interviews. Five of these interviews were for "manager trainee" positions with local companies and national corporations; two of these interviews were for administrative positions with large government agencies hiring for their expanding regional offices. All the job opportunities had good starting salaries and comprehensive benefit plans.

Jeff was hired by a regional telephone company as an accounting office supervisor. This was a first-line management position. Jeff had no formal training in business. He was part of a group of new hires that included five women and two men, all of whom had college degrees. Jeff later learned the company was under pressure to hire women for management-training positions. The company had been fined by the Equal Employment Opportunity Commission for paying male manager trainees more than female manager trainees for doing the same job in the 1960s. Jeff was assigned to the data processing unit, where he was trained to supervise 12 clerical employees processing daily service orders for the company. He saw his first computer, an IBM 360/60, which occupied a space the size of an executive office suite today.

Jeff acknowledges that there would be no way he would qualify for the same job opportunity right out of college today. Deregulation of the industry, technological changes, and fierce competition in the telecommunications industry have completely changed the hiring landscape in Jeff's organization.

Jeff's company is no longer looking for liberal arts graduates to train to "do it their way." His company is looking for a few select college graduates who can "hit the ground running." These candidates must have excellent grades in a business, finance, or computer information systems major and proven work experience in a corporate setting in order to qualify for an entry-level job comparable to the one Jeff was offered 35 years ago.

How can you help your child navigate this changed job market? If you can no longer assume that a college degree, any degree, will guarantee a foothold in today's economy, what can you do to help your child get focused?

Defining College Goals

You can start by getting your expectations out on the table. You can clarify in your own mind why you are sending your child to college in the first place. What does it mean to "find yourself" in college? How is this similar to or different from finding an initial career?

If you attended college, you may believe that "finding yourself" means expanding intellectually. You remember being inspired by dynamic instructors and energized by new ideas. Many college professors and other college personnel, most of whom liked school, share this definition of "finding yourself."

If you did not attend college, or if you dropped out, you may feel you were overlooked for career advancement because you lacked a college degree. You feel you were passed over for promotions because you didn't have "the piece of paper" to get ahead. You want your child to go to college to avoid your own employment fate.

You may think of "finding yourself" as a social experience. You remember college as the beginning of lifelong friendships. You want your child to make good friends in college and lay the groundwork for social and business networks later on.

You may define "finding yourself" as finding a cause or purpose in life. You remember college as a time of idealism and activism. College, for you, should be about energizing political discussions and collective social action.

You may see "finding yourself" as mastering independent life skills. You remember the sense of accomplishment that came from attending college away from home and meeting the challenges of getting along with roommates, balancing work and study, and managing money.

All of these are ways young people can and do find themselves in college. In an ideal college experience, one that develops the whole student, all of these self-discoveries take place.

But none of these experiences of finding yourself guarantees your child will find a good job. None of these expectations, if met, will assure that your child will leave college with the education and work experience needed to be marketable in a satisfying first career.

The fact is, few people find themselves, career-wise, in college. Ask any of your friends, "Are you working in your college field of study today?" Chances are they will laugh. Except for your friends who majored in professional majors like accounting, education, nursing, or pre-med, most of your friends did not find their career focus while in college. That happened later, by hit or miss, as your friends rolled out into the world and began their careers.

You need to move this process up in time to help your child get focused while he is in college and not just after graduation. Your child will enter a completely different economy than the one you and your friends entered back in the day. You cannot assume that your child will land on his feet just because he has a college degree. Without the right combination of education and relevant work experience, your child may leave college with few marketable skills and loaded with student-loan debt.

If your child is a strong student and you are reading this book, chances are you are well on your way to helping your child develop an academic plan. You took pride in your child's academic success in grade school and high school. You made sure your child signed up for honors courses and prepared for the SAT.

If your child is an average or weak student and you are reading this book, chances are you are worried about his success after high school. You want to do everything you can do now to help.

No matter what kind of student your child is in high school or college, now is the time to step back and spend the same amount of time you spent thinking about college preparedness thinking about career preparedness. If you want your child to find a satisfying first career, one that allows him to be financially independent and get on with adult life, you need to teach your child how to move from "undecided" and "unfocused" to "ready" and "prepared." This is true whether your child is an honors student or one who is "bored stiff" with high school.

Career success doesn't happen automatically. It doesn't happen without a plan. There are steps for getting from point A to point B. Your role as a parent is to be a resource to your child. Your job is to help your child identify other resources available to him that will move him forward into adult life.

So, if you believe it is OK for you to help your child with career planning, where do you begin? How do you help your child start the career-planning process in a constructive way?

Parent Tip 1

To be effective in helping your child with career planning, keep in mind the difference between guidance and control. Guidance is helping your child identify her strengths and connect those strengths to opportunities in the economy. Control is dictating your child's career choice. Guidance is helping your child get

(continued)

(continued)

firsthand information about the opportunities that are out there. Control is doing the research yourself. Guidance is saying, "I want you to talk to two engineers before you reject an engineering major." Control is saying, "I won't pay for college unless you major in engineering."

Parent Tip 2

Like most well meaning adults, you have probably asked your child, "What do you want to be when you grow up?" Because of this question, many young people resist any career-planning activities suggested by their parents. They fear they are being forced into making a choice they will be stuck with for the rest of their life. They feel they are being asked to decide, once and for all, what they are going to "be."

As a parent, you need to take the pressure off the career-planning process. You need to help your child separate career information gathering from career decision making. All you are asking your child to do at this point is gather information. You are not asking her to make a decision based on that information. Encourage your child to see herself as an objective journalist who is conducting research, interviewing people, and observing work environments. She can decide what she wants to do with this information later on.

Parent Tip 3

A college plan is not a career plan. "Where am I going to college?" and "How am I going to pay for it?" are different questions from "How am I going to support myself when I am out of college?"

In the past, a college plan was a career plan. Young adults could graduate from college and expect a college-level job with college-level pay just because they had a degree.

Times have changed. The economy has changed. Help your child develop a plan for an entry-level career after graduation. This career plan doesn't have to be in place on the front end of the college experience, but it can no longer wait until your child leaves college if you expect your child to pay back student loans.

A bachelor's degree does not entitle you to a dream job with good pay. It is an important first step on the road to a dream job with good pay. Help your child develop realistic expectations about employment after graduation and a workable plan to get established and get ahead.

CHAPTER 3

Getting Real About the 21st Century Job Market

The easiest and most effective way for you to help your child with career exploration is to encourage informational interviewing.

Here is how it works:

1. Using the Networking Contacts worksheet, write down the job titles or career fields your child has already considered in the Information About column.
2. Reviewing your own network of family, friends, and work associates, come up with the names of people working in the fields your child has indicated or in related fields.
3. Write the names of these contacts and their phone or e-mail information in the Name column on the Networking Contacts worksheet.
4. Help your child arrange a meeting with each of these people.
5. Have your child use the questions in "A Student's Guide to Informational Interviewing" as a guide for the conversation.
6. After each informational interview, have your child update the Networking Contacts worksheet.

NETWORKING CONTACTS

	Name	Phone/E-mail	Information About	√
1.	____________	____________	____________	___
2.	____________	____________	____________	___
3.	____________	____________	____________	___
4.	____________	____________	____________	___
5.	____________	____________	____________	___

A STUDENT'S GUIDE TO INFORMATIONAL INTERVIEWING

An informational interview is a conversation with someone who works in a career that interests you. The purpose of an informational interview is to gather firsthand information about the daily work and background of a person who is successful in a career you are considering. You should do informational interviews before you choose a major and begin preparing for a career.

To get informational interview contacts, make a list of all the people you know—parents, friends, relatives, co-workers, teachers, and more. Talk to each of them to get the names of people who work in the careers you are considering. Then use the following questions as a guide for your informational interview:

- What is your job title?
- What exactly do you do? What is your typical day like?
- What skills are necessary for someone in this field?
- What personal qualities are necessary for someone in this field?
- What do you like about your job?
- What do you dislike about your job?
- What education would I need to get into this field? What degrees, college major, training program, or special course would prepare me for this career?
- What are the entry-level jobs in the field?
- What work or volunteer experience would help me to get into this field?
- What is the starting salary and salary range for this job?
- Where is this field going in the next five to ten years?

- What are the job titles of some of the other people you work with?
- What are some other jobs you know of that require skills like yours?
- Do you know anyone else I could talk to about this career field?

How Informational Interviewing Can Help with Career Goals

Don't worry if your child's initial career goal seems unrealistic or out of reach. Most young people have an extremely limited view of what's "out there." Research suggests that most teenagers think they will enter one of 12 careers, most of which are in the professional ranks. These careers are doctor, lawyer, business executive, teacher, athlete, engineer, nurse, accountant, psychologist, architect, musician, and actor/director. Because these careers account for less than 20 percent of all jobs in the U.S. economy, with doctor and lawyer accounting for less that 1.3 percent of all jobs, many young people will not achieve their stated goal.

This does not mean they are doomed to a life of drudgery if they don't achieve their initial goal. It means they need to identify a wider range of careers. They need to develop a Plan B.

Informational interviews help your child do this. They help your child validate or reject an initial career idea. They lead to related career ideas for exploration. They provide information about the values important to your child and the activities that seem interesting. They expand your child's self-understanding by holding up a "mirror" of an adult who is working in a career day to day. They lead to new contacts for informational interviews.

Here is how the informational interview process played out for Megan:

"When I went to college, I didn't know what I wanted to do. I was interested in so many things—it was hard to choose. I thought about being a doctor and about being a teacher. I also thought about being a businesswoman.

"I started to talk to people about what they did for a living. I think my dad set up a couple of interviews for me in the beginning, and I just continued from there. I ruled out doctor because I decided that it would be hard to have kids with that kind of lifestyle. I thought about teaching, but after talking to several teachers it seemed like I wouldn't be learning enough new things on the job, that you kind of taught the same content each year with some variation.

"I really wanted to be a physician's assistant, but the college I was attending didn't have a program in that area. All the while I was talking to people, I kept taking those little career tests on the Internet that told you what you would be good at. I looked at Web sites that told you what the "hot" jobs were supposed to be in the next 10 years.

"Course-wise, I just took the basics my first year in college while I figured out what I wanted to do. By the first semester of my sophomore year in college, I still hadn't decided, so I sat down and asked myself, 'What have you learned about yourself in all your conversations so far? Is there anything that might combine all the things that interest you?'

"I kept coming back to speech therapy. I had talked to several speech therapists during my research. I knew that as a speech therapist I could work with a wide variety of people, from babies to the elderly. I would constantly be learning new things. I could work in clinical practice and later go on to teach if I wanted to or open my own business as a speech therapist. It looked like there would always be jobs in this field. While my income level would eventually plateau—I wasn't going to get rich as a speech therapist—it looked like I would always have a job, one that could be part-time when I had kids. So that's what I decided to do. I got a bachelor's degree in communication disorders and went on to get my master's.

"I think the key was just talking to lots and lots of people. All in all, it worked out for me really well."

Informational interviewing isn't rocket science. It's simply a matter of going out and talking to as many people as possible about different careers and seeing where those conversations lead next. Each informational interview will generate new ideas. It's like going to the public library and looking through the stacks. The books on either side of one you were looking for might be more interesting than your original selection.

In addition to directing your child to new career ideas, informational interviewing will give your child a more accurate view of the job market. This will enable her to make more informed decisions and you to control college costs.

What Does the Job Market Look Like?

Most young adults have a very one-sided picture of the job market. This view of the job market (Chart 1) shows them that education pays.

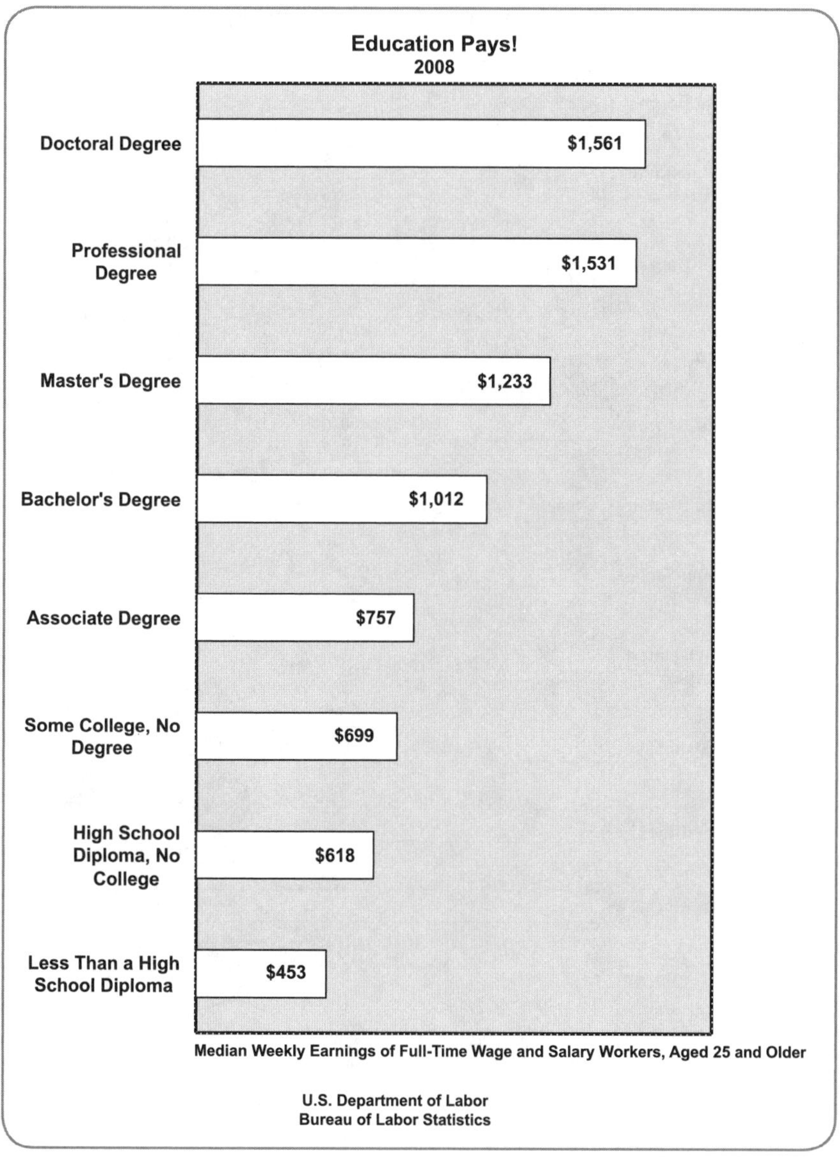

Chart 1: *Median weekly earnings of full-time workers, 2008.*

What young people don't have is a picture of the actual distribution of job openings in the U.S. economy by education and training level. Charts 2 and 3 show the actual distribution of jobs in the United States in 2008.

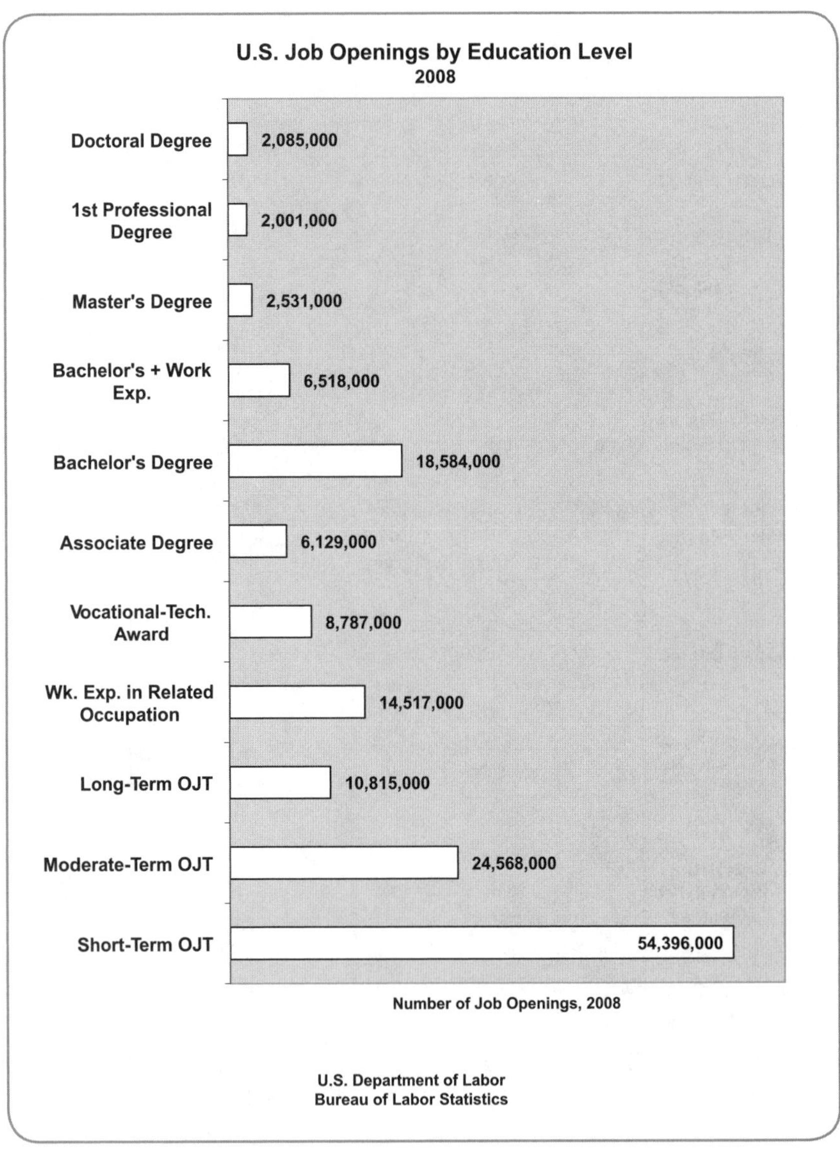

Chart 2: *U.S. jobs by education level, 2008.*

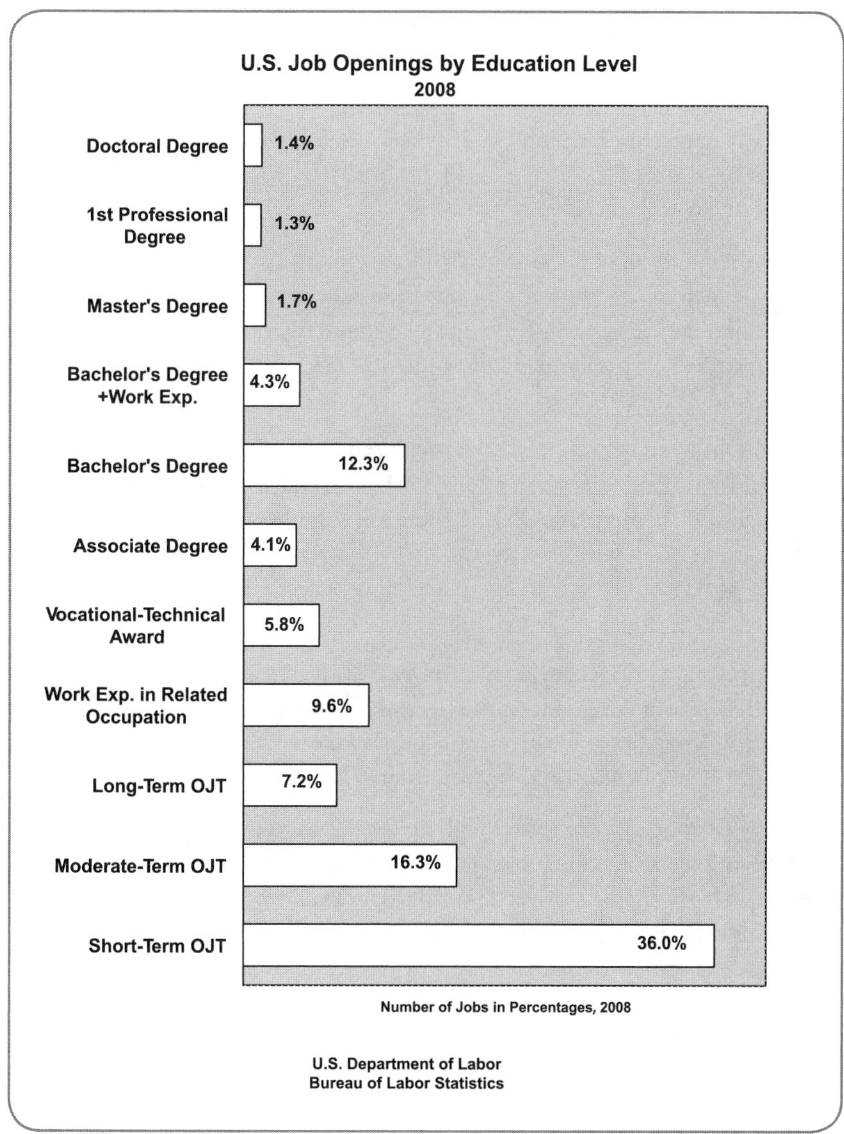

Chart 3: *U.S. job openings by education level in percentages, 2008.*

The fact is that 52 percent of all jobs in the United States in 2008 required only short-term (less than one month) to moderate-term (one to twelve months) informal or on-the-job training (OJT).

Another 26 percent of all jobs in 2008 required technical training ranging from long-term OJT (1–5 years OJT, in-house training, or apprenticeship) to an associate degree.

Twenty-one percent of all jobs in 2008 required a bachelor's degree or higher. Less than 4.5 percent of jobs required a master's degree or higher. The median earnings of all full-time U.S. workers in 2008 were $32,390 per year, or $15.57 per hour. Half of all workers made more than this amount and half made less.

Both you and your child need to understand that this is the job market your child will face. Only then will you be able to help your child make realistic and effective plans. While there are many exciting career opportunities today, they will be open only to young people with the right combination of education, work experience, and people skills to do the jobs employers want done.

It is important to understand that the BLS Jobs by Education Level data on in 2008 reflects the education and training that the BLS and industry experts say is necessary for proficient performance of the job. It does not reflect the level of education of people actually doing the job.

The level of education of individual workers is sometimes higher and sometimes lower than the job requires. An example would be a computer programmer (bachelor's degree training required) who entered the computer field 25 years ago without a degree and worked up through the ranks. At the same time, a bachelor's degree computer programmer whose job was shipped to India in 2001 may now be working as a sales clerk in a home improvement store. This job requires only short-term OJT. According to the 2008 BLS data, more than 6.3 million adults with a bachelor's degree or higher were working in jobs requiring only short-term OJT. This is called "underemployment."

Chances are the distribution of jobs presented in Chart 2 is not what you expected. With all the pressure on young people to get a college degree, you probably expected more bachelor's degree jobs to be out there. You have watched well-paying manufacturing jobs being shipped overseas or eliminated by technology over the past 25 years, and you have placed your hopes for your child achieving a middle-class lifestyle on her earning a four-year bachelor's degree. And you are willing to borrow increasingly large sums of money to help your child achieve this goal.

The truth is that many young people who start college leave without achieving their stated educational goal. Seventy percent of high school graduates enroll in college within two years of graduating from high school. Most of these students intend to get a bachelor's degree or higher. More than half of all students who start college leave without completing a degree or certificate. At a community college, the number of students who leave without earning a degree or certificate can climb as high as 75 percent. Many young adults, especially those without a career plan or focus, will try college, drop out, and drift down into the economy. They will end up working in jobs requiring only short-term or moderate-term OJT because this is where the majority of jobs are.

What can you, as a parent, do to help your child achieve a positive outcome after high school?

You can encourage your child to spend as much time researching careers and industries as researching colleges. You can help your child gather accurate, real-world information to inform her decisions. You can help her connect with people who work in a variety of careers and industries to find out what is going on. The easiest way to do this is through informational interviewing.

Identifying Your Career Connections

How do you go about finding people for your child to talk to in an informational interview?

You tap into your own network of contacts. You identify the networking contacts you already have and help your child make career connections with those contacts.

Networking as a job-search strategy addresses the fact that 70 percent of jobs available at any given time are never advertised in traditional forums, such as newspaper want ads or career/job Web sites. Most jobs are found by word of mouth, or networking. To network in the job-search process means to get your name and qualifications out there to as many people as possible so that those people think of you when "hidden" jobs open up.

Networking in the career-planning process for young people works the same way. Just as many good jobs are "hidden" from adult job seekers, many good career paths are hidden from young adults. Networking is the way your child can generate career ideas that are not readily apparent when using the traditional method of choosing a career, which in the United States is "choose a college major and hope for the best."

You may find the idea of networking intimidating at first. If you haven't had to look for a job recently, you may think networking is beyond your ability. But networking is just a structured way of getting and giving information about jobs and careers.

Everyone has a network. To understand your own network, think of eight working adults you know. These people can be family members, friends, co-workers, or neighbors—anyone you are comfortable talking with on an informal basis. Write the names of these people on the My Network worksheet. Complete the worksheet with information about each person.

My Network

Name	Phone/ E-mail	Job Title	Company/ Organization	Industry/ Sector

The following worksheet shows you Jeff's network.

Name	Phone/ E-mail	Job Title	Company/ Organization	Industry/ Sector
Keith Hastings	816-316-1977 hastingsk@mwlease.com	Owner/ Manager	Midwest Equipment Leasing	Financial Services
Jane Elliott	816-731-2004 elliottj@swrmc.org	Human Resources Manager	Southwestern Medical Center	Health Care
Clayton Parker	816-616-1931 cparker@reachout.org	Executive Director	Reach Out	Not-for-Profit
Elizabeth Sayers	816-195-1707 esayers@marple.com	Graphic Designer	The Marple Agency	Advertising
Albert Robinson	816-304-1987 robinsona@rad.com	Corporate Attorney	Robinson, Allen, and Dube, P.C.	Legal Services
Lily McGuire	417-404-4200 lilianm@sps.K12.edu	Elementary School Teacher	Springfield Public Schools	K–12 Education
Greg Bredon	660-308-1951 gbredon@bunter.com	Mechanical Engineer	Bunter Engineering, Inc.	Engineering Consulting
Dave Bantry	913-822-1979 dbantry@ecc.com	Project Manager	Electrical Supply Company	Construction

Keith is the owner and sales manager of Midwest Equipment Leasing Company. Keith can give Jeff specific information about

- The job duties of a sales manager.
- How to run a successful small business.
- The equipment leasing industry in general.
- Sales as a profession.
- The financial services sector of the economy.
- Where the leasing equipment industry is going in the future.

- The specific education and work experience Jeff would need to get into the leasing industry.
- The job titles and duties of other employees at Midwest Equipment Leasing.
- How Jeff could get hired at Midwest Equipment Leasing Company.

Jane is the human resources manager for a large regional medical center. Jane can give Jeff specific information about

- Her job duties as an HR manager.
- The names of people working in a variety of other health care careers, including nursing, respiratory therapy, hospital administration, physical therapy, and so on.
- The field of human resources in general.
- Trends in hospital administration.
- Whether Southwestern Medical Center is hiring.
- How Jeff could get a job or an internship at Southwestern Medical Center.
- The names of other HR managers in the area who are members of her professional organization.

Clayton is the executive director of Reach Out, a non-profit agency working with the elderly poor. Clayton can give Jeff information about

- The role of an executive director in a non-profit agency.
- The field of social services in general.
- The not-for-profit sector of the economy.
- The different kinds of jobs that are part of an agency such as Reach Out.
- Contacts with other people working in social services.
- How to revise his resume to make it more effective.

Keith, Jane, and Clayton are all part of Jeff's network.

Everyone has a network. If you identify the members of your network, they can provide informational interviews for your child. They can help your child brainstorm career ideas and uncover additional job titles to research.

Members of your network can provide your child with three kinds of interviews that are part of the job-search process. These include informal interviews, informational interviews, and job interviews.

Informal interviews are conversations with family and friends to brainstorm ideas and get job leads. The purpose of an informal interview is to get ideas and get the names of people to talk to. These new contacts can help your child explore a career, identify a career objective, or find out how to get hired at a particular company.

Informational interviews are more structured conversations than informal interviews. They are designed to help your child get specific, firsthand information about a career or about the company a person works for. The purpose of an informational interview is to get information. It is not to get a job. An informational interview will give your child accurate, detailed information about a career, as well as suggestions for people to talk to next.

A job interview is a formal interview in which your child sells her skills and qualifications for a particular job. A successful job interview requires that your child know her skills and how to communicate them both verbally and on a resume. It requires that she know how her skills will benefit the employer. The informal and informational interviews your child conducts before a job interview will increase her ability to sell herself in a job interview and get the job she wants.

Ultimately, your child will decide where she wants to land on the economic ladder. Informational interviews will help her identify the education and work experience she will need to be successful at whatever goal she chooses for herself.

But what if you want more ideas for your child to research than her initial informational interviews provide? Isn't there a test that can tell your child what to do?

Parent Tip 4

It is not your job to decide the merits of your child's career ideas. It is your job to facilitate the information gathering. To be effective in your role, you need to get out of power struggles with your child over career decisions. Informational interviews help you do that. They let your child do a reality check on her career ideas with someone other than you. They let life be the teacher. Your job is to let the teaching happen.

Parent Tip 5

One way to ease into the informational-interview process is to have your child conduct an informational interview with you. Most young people are relatively clueless about what their parents do for a living. Sit down with your child and have her ask you the informational interview questions in the beginning of this chapter. This will break the ice on the informational-interview process. Let your child role-play an informational interview before going "live" with someone new.

Parent Tip 6

One thing that sometimes holds parents back from encouraging career exploration is the unspoken fear that their child's initial goal is unrealistic. Some parents secretly think that an unrealistic goal is better than no goal at all.

If you know your child doesn't have the math skills or motivation to become a pharmacist or engineer, is there something more constructive you can do than send him off to college, knowing he will fail?

Encourage your child to begin career research early. Career research can, and should, begin in high school. This research will help your child evaluate an initial goal and move on, if necessary, to other, more achievable goals.

Every student, even the most gifted and talented, needs a Plan B. Life happens. By engaging in career research early, your child can identify several career paths and have a Plan B ready if Plan A doesn't work out.

Parent Tip 7

Looking at the distribution of jobs by education and training level in Chart 2, you may be wondering why everyone, including teachers, counselors, parents, politicians, and the media, is telling all high school students they need a college degree to be successful.

Even if every high school graduate in the U.S. earned a four-year college degree, the percentage of jobs requiring a bachelor's degree for entry into the career would still be only 12.3 percent. And if all those college graduates went on to pursue a master's degree, that wouldn't change the fact that only 1.7 percent of all jobs require one.

Part of the problem is that many people simply aren't aware of the actual distribution of jobs in the labor market. They are often shocked to realize that more than 52 percent of jobs in the U.S. require less than one year of on-the job training.

In addition, many people do not differentiate between job openings due to growth and job openings due to replacement needs. Job growth reflects newly created job openings that did not exist before. Job replacement reflects job openings due to workers leaving existing jobs. Job openings from replacement needs are projected to be more than double the numbers of job openings due to economic growth between 2008 and 2018.

Finally, as well-paying manufacturing jobs disappeared over the last 25 years, many people came to believe that a college degree is the only sure route to a comfortable and financially sound life in the middle class. Even this deeply held belief has been challenged in recent years as hundreds of thousands of white-collar workers with college degrees lost well-paying jobs during the recession.

All of this raises some important questions, such as What is a college degree? What is middle class?

There are many paths to a postsecondary education these days: traditional colleges and universities, community colleges, proprietary schools, career/technical centers, and online programs of all types. And with a wide array of economic outcomes for each educational credential, it's clear you need to think long and hard about the kind of education and lifestyle you want for your child. Rather than tell your child, "A college degree is the door to the middle class," point out that developing marketable skills is how people become financially successful in life. This is true whether their educational credential is a certificate in wind energy technology or a master's degree in social work.

(continued)

(continued)

By emphasizing skills, you are able to make better decisions about how to spend and stretch your educational dollars. Marketable skills can be acquired through a variety of educational and training venues, including a four-year college or university, a community college, a proprietary school, a career or technical training school, work experience, graduate school, and the military. You need to teach your child that acquiring skills is not a one-time, one-shot event signified by earning a degree or certificate. Rather, it is a lifelong learning process in which each new job and life experience offers an opportunity to learn more skills and make new contacts.

Parent Tip 8

In times of economic downturn, it is easy to lose sight of the fact that there are still people who are employed, and these people are a valuable source of information about which jobs will be available for entry-level workers when the economy loosens up.

People you know who are employed are part of your network. One of the most helpful things you can do is encourage your child to meet with members of your network to identify the skills, education, and work experience needed to be marketable in a variety of entry-level jobs in different sectors of the economy.

Identify one person you know who has a job. This person is a potential resource to your child about a variety of career-related topics, including the day-to-day duties of the job, the education and work experience needed to be hired for an entry-level position, the pathways to better-paying jobs in this career field, and the "big picture" with regard to the future of this job and industry in a global economy.

Don't forget you have a network, even in tough economic times. Use your network to help your child connect with information and opportunities.

CHAPTER 4

Assessing for Strengths; Researching and Interviewing for Information

There is no one test that can tell your child what to be. But there are a number of career-interest inventories available in print and online to help you guide your child with career planning.

What Is a Career-Interest Inventory?

A career-interest inventory is a questionnaire your child completes to identify the pattern of his interests according to the framework of the test. Your child answers a series of questions about school subjects, activities, occupations of interest, and other preferences. The answers are scored and your child receives an interpretative report that includes a list of job titles. These job titles provide a starting point for career research.

Career-interest inventories take a "birds of a feather flock together" approach to career planning. The idea is that if your child has interests similar to someone working in a particular field, such as accounting, your child might enjoy being around accountants. He can add "accountant" to his Networking Contacts list and research this career by reading about it on the Internet and conducting informational interviews with accountants.

Your goal in encouraging your child to take an interest inventory is to help him identify job titles for initial career research. Your goal is not to persuade your child to choose the career you would like him to choose. Nor is it to pressure your child into choosing the career you wish you had chosen 25 years ago.

A career-interest inventory tells your child to "start here" based on his own interests and preferences. By reading about the careers reflected on the inventory and talking to people in the field, your child will go beyond the initial job titles listed on the inventory and identify related careers that might be a good fit.

How do you go about having your child take a career inventory?

If your child is in college, have him go to the college counseling or career center and get help there. Most colleges offer a variety of career resources, which are often underutilized by students. A good time for your child to check out these career resources is second semester of freshman year. By this time, your child will be over the initial excitement of living away from home, adjusted to the higher academic expectations of college, and starting to feel some anxiety about career and major issues. After all, his goal for the past 18 years has been getting into college. What happens next?

In the career center, your child will be offered a number of popular career inventories from which to choose, including the Strong Interest Inventory (SII), the Self-Directed Search (SDS), the Career Information System (CIS), the CHOICES Interest Profiler, the DISCOVER Interest Inventory, and many other excellent assessments. He may be encouraged to take other personality, skills, or values inventories as well.

The interest inventory your child takes isn't important. There are many excellent products on the market and available on the Internet for a fee. The important part is helping your child understand the results. Encourage your child to follow through on the next steps of career exploration, which are reading about the careers on the Internet and talking to people in the field.

Personality Type and Satisfying Careers

One of the most popular frameworks for career-interest inventories used with high school and college students is psychologist John Holland's theory of personality. Many career inventories use the Holland framework, including the Strong Interest Inventory, the Self-Directed Search, the ACT (UNAICT) Interest Inventory, the KUDER Career Search with Person Match, and the U.S. Government's O*NET Interest Profiler. Because Holland's theory is so widely used in career planning, it is helpful for you, as a parent, to understand his ideas.

Holland's theory is that occupational choice is an expression of personality. "Personality" is the pattern of an individual's values, interests, skills, attitudes, and behaviors. According to Holland, personality preferences are shaped through environmental influences, genetic makeup, and the experiences of early life. By the age of 21, according to Holland, people's personality preferences are fairly set. The things that engage a person's interest at 21 will be similar to those that engage that person's interest at 60.

Holland's theory is that there are six basic personality types and six corresponding work environments. The hexagon in Figure 1 is used to illustrate the Holland theory.

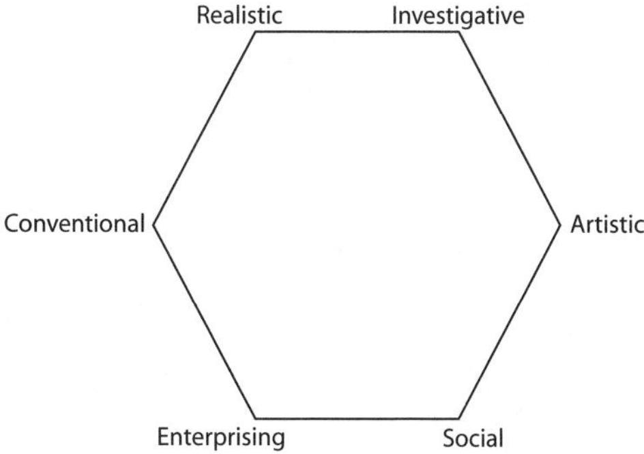

Figure 1: *A hexagon represents Holland's theory of personality types and work environments.*

Realistic—People who have athletic or mechanical ability and who prefer to work with objects, machines, tools, plants, or animals or to be outdoors. They have a preference for working with things as opposed to ideas or people and prefer concrete problems over abstract problems.

Investigative—People who like to observe, learn, investigate, analyze, evaluate, or solve problems primarily of a scientific or mathematical nature. They prefer working with ideas as opposed to people and do not like highly structured settings.

Artistic—People who have artistic, innovative, or intuitional abilities and who like to work in unstructured situations, using their creativity or imagination. They prefer working with self-expressive ideas.

(continued)

(continued)

Social—People who like to work with people to inform, enlighten, help, train, or cure them or help them live up to their potential. They prefer solving problems through discussion and usually do not prefer working with things.

Enterprising—People who like to work with people, influencing, persuading, leading, or managing them for economic gain or for the goals of an organization. They enjoy leadership positions and dislike details.

Conventional—People who like to work with data, have clerical or numerical ability, and enjoy carrying things out in detail or following through on others' instructions. They prefer structured situations over ambiguous ones.

According to Holland, each person is a unique combination of personality types, but usually two or three of the types are dominant. Holland's theory is that if you can identify your personality type, you can match it to work environments that reward and validate your personality type. The implication is that you will be happier, more productive, and more successful in a work environment that matches your personality type and allows you to work with people who share a similar pattern of interest.

So far, so good. Holland's hexagon is easy to understand. There are well-researched connections between the six points of the hexagon. People readily see themselves in two or three of the Holland types. Career inventories based on Holland give your child job titles rooted in the pattern of responses your child made on the Holland-based career inventory he completed. They give you and your child direction to industries and organizations to explore. They suggest zones of the economy for research. Holland-based inventories provide an excellent starting point for career research.

But it is important to understand that the results of any Holland-based career inventory are presented according to a theory of personality and not according to the actual distribution of jobs in the labor market. Holland's theory is a personality theory, not a model of the U.S. job market. In the real world, jobs are not evenly distributed according to Holland type. Visually, the Holland hexagon suggests to students that there are an equal number of careers in each of the six corners of the hexagon. The message is "Just identify your personality type and there will be plenty of jobs available."

You, as a working adult, know this is incorrect. You know jobs are not distributed by Holland types.

So, what does the job market look like?

Florida State University counselors studied U.S. census data over a 40-year period, 1960–2000. They determined that in the year 2000, jobs were distributed this way:

- 30 percent of jobs were Realistic.
- 8 percent of jobs were Investigative.
- 1 percent of jobs were Artistic.
- 16 percent of jobs were Social.
- 30 percent of jobs were Enterprising.
- 15 percent of jobs were Conventional.

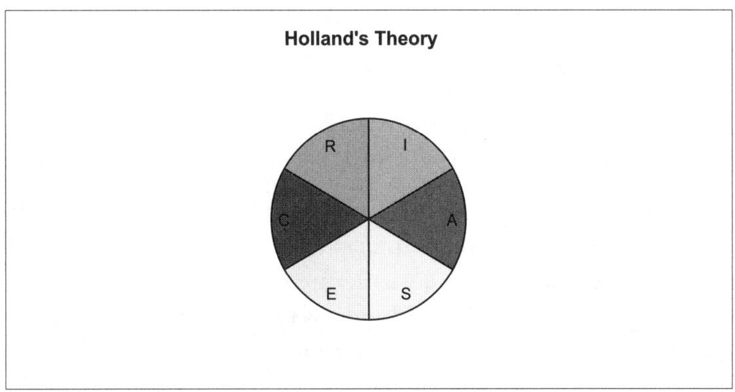

Figure 2: *Visually, students see Holland's types as balanced.*

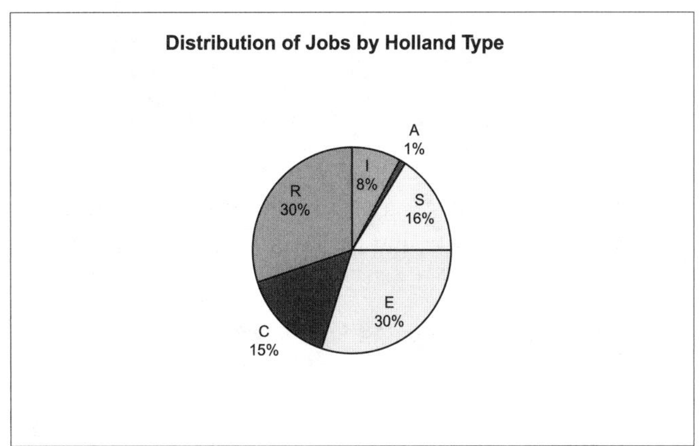

Figure 3: *The actual distribution of jobs is imbalanced.*

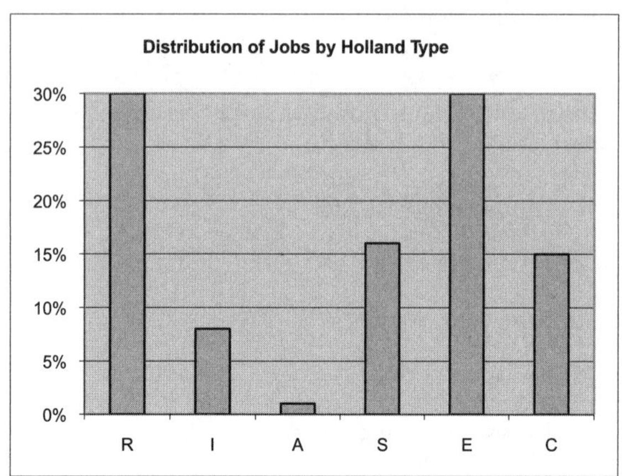

Figure 4: *Another way to view the distribution of jobs by Holland type.*

The FSU research suggests that 75 percent of all jobs in the U.S. economy fall into three Holland areas: Enterprising, Realistic, and Conventional. Only 1 percent of jobs fall into the Artistic area, 8 percent into the Investigative area, and 16 percent into the Social area.

Your child needs to be aware of the distribution of jobs in the labor market. He needs to have an accurate understanding of how the job market is structured because it is within this structure that he must find something interesting to do. The number and kinds of jobs available at any given time are determined by the demand for goods and services, not by the personality types of the people looking for work.

In addition to showing how jobs are distributed, the Florida State researchers noted some shifts in employment by Holland code over 40 years:

- Employment in the Realistic area declined by 25 percent from 1960 to 2000, but it still remains the largest area of employment. The number of Realistic jobs actually increased in real numbers from 1960 to 2000.
- Employment in the Investigative area increased by 5 percent, Social by 7 percent, and Enterprising by 13 percent between 1960 and 2000.
- Employment in the Artistic and Conventional areas remained stable.

- The largest area of employment in terms of number of jobs in 2000 was Realistic, followed in order by Enterprising, Social, Conventional, Investigative and Artistic.
- The highest annual income for jobs was in Investigative, followed by Enterprising, Social, Artistic, Realistic and Conventional.

What does all this mean? It means your child needs some help interpreting any career inventories he takes in order to put the information into perspective. At the college level, that assistance is provided in the career or counseling center. You can provide assistance as well. You can direct your child to Internet resources and provide networking contacts so your child can talk to people in the field.

Finding Web Resources for Career Planning

Now, what about Internet research? How can you help your child get started?

Keep it simple. The easiest place for most people to start is the *Occupational Outlook Handbook*. This is the U.S. government's database of occupational information. To find it, search for "Occupational Outlook Handbook Online" or go to www.bls.gov/oco. The *OOH* is also available in hard copy at any public library.

The *OOH* provides information on hundreds of specific job titles. It provides links from general areas of the economy, such as management, professional, service, sales, administrative, farming, construction, installation, production, transportation, and armed forces, to specific job titles in those areas.

In the *OOH*, your child can read articles about a myriad of careers. Each article gives a broad outline of the job duties, education, salary, and job outlook for each career. At the end of most of the articles in the *OOH* is a section called "Related Occupations." Here your child will find links to additional job titles to research.

Researching careers on the Internet is simple:

1. Have your child list the careers suggested by any interest inventory under "Information About" on the Networking Contacts worksheet in Chapter 3.

2. Have your child spend an hour researching these careers on the Web, using the *OOH* Web site.
3. Have your child write down each related career that seems interesting.
4. Based on Internet research, have your child identify the careers he wants to research further.
5. Help your child set up informational interviews with people working in the careers that have risen to the top of his Networking Contacts list.

Here are a few cautions about interpreting occupational information your child finds on the Internet or in print media:

- Occupational statistics are sometimes presented in percentages and sometimes presented in numbers of people employed. To interpret any "increase" or "decrease" in number of jobs correctly, you need to know whether the change is a percentage change or a numerical change.

  A high percentage increase in a job can actually mean a small increase in the numbers of jobs, while a large number of jobs can be available despite a decline in the percentage of jobs.

  Here is an example:

  Employment of physician's assistants is expected to grow 39 percent from 2008 to 2018, much faster than the average for all occupations.

  The numerical increase of physician's assistants will be 29,100 jobs. The number of physician's assistants working in the U.S. will increase from 74,800 in 2008 to 103,900 in 2018.

  In contrast, employment of machinists is projected to decline by 4.6 percent over the 2008–2018 decade. Even with a decline of 19,300 jobs over 10 years, however, it is still projected that there will be 402,200 machinist jobs in 2018.

  This means there will be 298,300 more machinist jobs than physician's assistant jobs in 2018, even though machinist jobs are expected to decline by 4.6 percent and physician's assistant jobs are expected to increase by 39 percent over the 10-year period.

- You need to consider both new jobs and replacement jobs when thinking about employment growth. More job openings stem from replacement needs than from the addition of new jobs.

To understand this, imagine your community has 10 urologists (education level: first professional degree of M.D. with a specialty in urology) and 100 plumbers (education level: long-term on-the-job training.) The government tells you to expect a 10 percent growth in urologist jobs over the next 10 years and a 2 percent increase in plumber jobs. You run the numbers and note that there will be one additional urologist job and two additional plumber jobs added to the total number of jobs in your community over the next 10 years.

The government also tells you that half of all current jobs in both groups—urologists and plumbers—will need to be replaced by new workers in the next 10 years as baby boomers retire. This means there will be an additional five urologist jobs opening up, along with an additional 50 plumber jobs. When these replacement jobs are added to the newly created jobs, the total number of job opportunities for urologists over the next 10 years will be six, while the total number of job opportunities for plumbers will be 52.

- When reading about growth in sectors of the economy like health care or computers, it is important to determine which jobs within the sector are being discussed.

  If you read an article that says "Health-Care Careers Up 30 Percent," you need to look beyond the percentage increase and find out what is really going on within the various levels of jobs that coexist in that sector of economy. How many additional doctors versus home health aides does a 30 percent rise in health-care jobs include?

  A 30 percent increase in health-care jobs over 10 years, reflected in numbers rather than percentages, might include the following job distributions:

Projected numerical increase	Percentage increase
460,900 more home health aides	50 percent
29,200 more physician's assistants	39 percent
581,500 more registered nurses	22 percent
144,100 more doctors	22 percent

This distribution of jobs within a sector of the economy makes a difference to your child's career planning. It determines the competition your child will face getting into academic programs and the ease with which your child will find employment.

- Occupational projections vary in certainty. Some projections like "There will be a greater demand for health-care services as baby boomers age" are a sure thing. But other projections are not so sure.

  The projection that "All full-time, master's-degreed reference librarians who retire in the next 15 years will be replaced with full-time, master's-degreed reference librarians" may or may not prove true.

  Many variables could impact the job market for librarians. Technology could change library services. In fact, much of the increased productivity the U.S. has experienced overall in recent years has been a result of doing more with less. Companies have become more productive by adding duties to existing staff members rather than hiring new employees or replacing those who retire. This could happen in libraries.

  Funding cuts in education could result in more part-time librarians. Fewer librarians could retire due to economic fears. Libraries could create library-manager positions and hire people with less education for less pay to assume some of the supervisory tasks performed by master's-level librarians.

  The only way to identify these trends is to talk to people in the field. There is no substitute for informational interviewing. To select a career without doing informational interviews is like buying a car without driving it around the block. If you end up with a lemon, it is your own fault.

- Occupational projections are based on the idea that the past can predict the future. In a global economy, however, occupational changes are increasingly difficult to predict.

  Few analysts in 1960 predicted that women in the 1970s would enter the workforce in large numbers and stay there. Few analysts in 1970 predicted that the creation of digitized computer files would allow millions of American jobs to be performed by engineers, accountants, and computer programmers working in other countries.

  The only way to find out the global implications for a career is to talk to people currently working in the field. This is the only way to identify the good jobs of the future. Using career-test results to do

> Internet research is an excellent starting point for career planning, but it is essential that your child talk to people in the field to find out exactly where a career or industry is going.

Now that your child has taken some career assessments and done some informational interviews, what if you want more ideas for career planning? Is there another approach you can take to help your child identify potential careers?

Parent Tip 9

If your child is in high school, she may already have some career inventory results on file. Many students complete a series of tests in middle school and high school that include interest inventories. The ACT PLAN test is one such test. It is often administered to high school sophomores. The PLAN suggests career paths for exploration, as well as giving students a reality check about their college preparedness.

The ACT test is another test that includes an interest inventory. The ACT is taken by many high school students as part of the college application process. It includes a well-researched career inventory that will give you, as a parent, a baseline reading of your child's career interests. It will give you and your child specific job titles to research, as well as specific majors to explore.

Most parents are so focused on their child's ACT scores and the implication of those scores for college admission that they overlook the valuable career information reflected on the ACT summary report. In particular, the ACT can direct you and your child to specific career areas that match the interests your child indicated on the test, as well as to specific job titles to research and majors to explore.

Find out what career tests your child has already taken at the high school level. Use them to encourage your child's career exploration.

Parent Tip 10

While there are a few highly motivated students who find career research fascinating, most young people won't do career research unless they have to. Sifting through the kind of print career information currently on the Internet can be pretty dull. Some Web sites offer video clips, but these Web sites can be difficult to find. But career research is important. Your child's career and educational decisions will only be as good as the data that goes into them. Have your child make a project out of career research in the same way that she makes a project out of choosing a college.

(continued)

(continued)

As part of the college-selection process, have her complete three Just the Facts worksheets. Using career titles listed on her Networking Contacts list worksheet (see Chapter 3), have your child research each of these careers on the Internet, answering all the questions on the Just the Facts worksheet.

Sit down with your child and talk about her research. In particular, listen to your child's response to the last question: "After researching this career, are you still interested in it? Why or why not?"

The answer will give you valuable insights into the values, interests, and skills that are shaping your child's decision making.

JUST THE FACTS!

1. Career/job title: ____________________
2. Job description: ____________________

   ____
3. Salary: ____________________
4. Outlook (will there be jobs in the future?) ____________________

   ____
5. Educational requirements: ____________________
6. If a college degree is required, what is the college major? ____________________
7. Related occupations: ____________________

   ____
8. Sources for more information: ____________________

   ____
9. After researching this career, are you still interested in it? Why or why not?

   ____

CHAPTER 5

Turning Talents and Skills into Jobs and Careers

Chances are you have told your child, "Do what interests you!" But what does it mean to "do something you like"? How is your child supposed to figure this out?

Finding a First Career

There are two basic ways to find an initial career. One is to look at what already interests you and see if you want to make a career out of that. The other is to think about the skills you enjoy using and find something interesting to do with those skills.

Here is an example of the second approach:

Matt is interested in music. He has played guitar and drums since he was 12. He organized several rock bands while in high school. He likes to write music and perform rock music on the stage.

If Matt wants to make a career out of his interest in music, he can take his band on the road, play music in various venues, and find out how far he can go with performing his music. If he is truly passionate about it, he can support himself with other jobs to allow himself the freedom to pursue his chosen career as a musician. But if Matt decides that he does not want to be a rock musician or that he does not have the talent to make a living as a rock musician, he can explore other careers that relate to his interest in music.

If Matt has good hands-on skills with building, fixing, and repairing things, he can investigate a career repairing musical instruments. He could apprentice as a luthier in a music repair shop and make his living repairing guitars.

If Matt has good math skills and enjoys solving scientific and mathematical problems, he could become a sound engineer and design sound systems for concert halls and amphitheaters.

If Matt can write well, he could become a music reviewer for a newspaper or magazine. If he has good teaching skills and enjoys communicating his enthusiasm for music to others, he could become a music teacher.

If Matt has good business skills, he could apply them to the business side of music. If he is good at managing, marketing, and promoting, he could become a band manager. If he is good at clerical detail and using the computer, he could work as an inventory-control clerk for a store that sells percussion instruments to bands.

Or Matt could find an interesting job in something completely unrelated to music. He could use his business skills to open a coffee shop in the arts district downtown. He could use his skills in another area of the economy besides the music industry and save his music for his free time. This is called career/life balance. Not every interest and skill has to be part of Matt's paid employment for him to still enjoy his work.

Through this simple brainstorming exercise, Matt identified six careers to research:

- Musician
- Luthier
- Audio Engineer
- Music Reviewer
- Music Teacher
- Band Manager

Matt can add these job titles to his Networking Contacts list (see Chapter 3), and his parents can identify people they know who work in these careers or related careers. Matt can set up some informational interviews.

Here is another example:

Tania is interested in biology. She enjoys working with a microscope and setting up lab experiments in school.

If she has good math-problem solving and research skills, she could consider a career as a biologist, perhaps working in a cancer institute developing treatments for cancer.

If Tania has good hands-on skills like building, repairing, and fixing things, she could consider a career as a biomedical-equipment technician. She could train to work on medical equipment such as defibrillators, heart monitors, and medical imaging equipment.

If Tania has good artistic skills and enjoys writing, drawing, and designing, she could work as an illustrator for a company that publishes medical textbooks.

If she enjoys teaching, training, and instructing people, she could become a biology teacher.

If she has good sales skills and is able to sell, persuade, and promote products, she could become a pharmaceutical rep.

And if she has good organization and clerical-detail skills, she could become a pharmacy technician.

Or Tania could do something completely unrelated to biology. Based on the limited jobs available in her small Midwestern town, she could go to work as a personal banker, using her communication and clerical-detail skills to earn a living. She could volunteer with the local clean-waterways organization on the weekends and spend her free time preserving the environment in her community. This is career/life balance.

Tania has identified six careers to research:

- Biologist
- Biomedical-Equipment Technician
- Medical Illustrator
- Biology Teacher
- Pharmaceutical Rep
- Pharmacy Technician

Tania can add these jobs to her Networking Contacts list (see Chapter 3) and enlist her parents' help to identify people working in these careers or related careers and conduct informational interviews with them.

Here is a third example:

Jack loves golf. He plays golf on the high school golf team and works at a golf course during the summer. Jack can look at his skills and see whether he can make a career of them in his field of interest, which is golf.

He could become a golf pro and see if he could make a living playing golf professionally.

He could work outdoors growing, maintaining, and landscaping golf courses. He could become a grounds and turf manager at a golf club.

He could research and design more-efficient golf equipment. He could become a research and development engineer for a golf-equipment manufacturer.

He could design golf courses, working as a landscape architect.

He could write about golf as a sports journalist covering the pro golf circuit.

He could manage a pro shop or become an operations manager of a country club.

He could work as a retail-sales clerk in a golf pro shop.

Or Jack could do something completely unrelated to golf as his paid employment. He could become an accountant and play golf in his free time. He could vacation at Pebble Beach and play the golf course there. This is career/life balance.

Jack has now identified seven job titles to research:

- Professional Golfer
- Grounds and Turf Manager
- Research and Development Engineer
- Landscape Architect
- Sports Journalist
- Pro Shop Manager
- Pro Shop Clerk

All of the examples in this section take a subject of interest (a noun, such as music, biology, or golf) and combine it with a cluster of skills (verbs) to come up with different career directions for exploration. These are the six skills clusters:

Build, repair, fix, work outdoors

Research, analyze, solve math and science problems

Draw, compose, write, act, perform

Teach, train, care for others

Manage, sell, motivate, persuade

Organize information, process information, verify accuracy

If these skill sets sound familiar, they should. They are grouped according to the Holland theory discussed in Chapter 4. These skills are called functional or transferable skills.

The Skills Pyramid

Functional skills are one of three kinds of skills necessary for the performance of any job. Figure 1 shows the three kinds of skills.

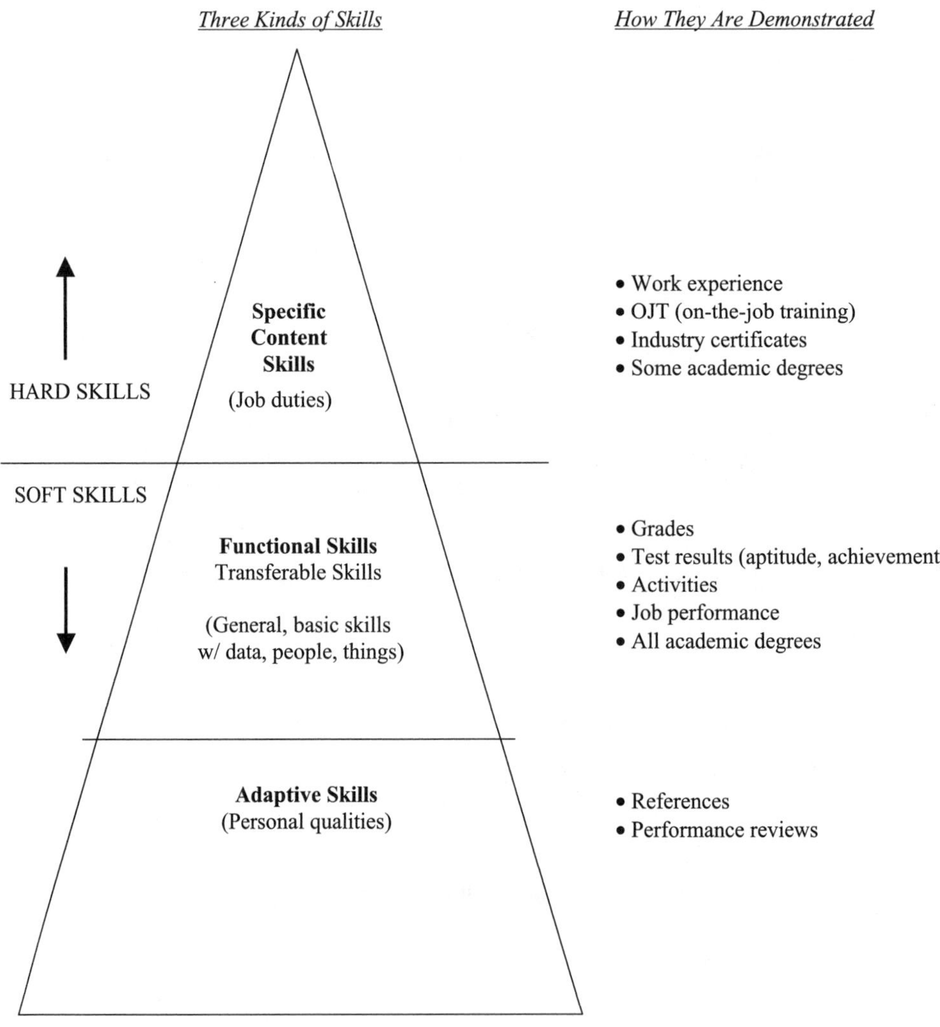

Figure 1: *The skills pyramid.*

Adaptive Skills

At the foundation of the skills pyramid are adaptive skills. Adaptive skills are "self-management" skills. They describe the personal skills a person brings to a job that enable her to adapt to the particular work environment.

Adaptive skills are often described as personal qualities such as "dependability," "honesty," "courtesy," and "reliability." They are sometimes lumped together under the umbrella term of "work ethic."

People often overlook adaptive skills when they think about their skills. Adaptive skills are seen as attributes of the person rather than skills the person developed over time.

In reality, adaptive skills are made up of a series of behaviors. Some of the behaviors connected with different adaptive skills are shown on the Adaptive Skills Checklist.

ADAPTIVE SKILLS CHECKLIST

Adaptive Skill	Behaviors	Rating (1–5)
Cheerful	Are you generally in a good mood? Do you greet your co-workers pleasantly?	
Conscientious	Do you do an honest day's work for a day's pay? Can you name an unpleasant work task you have done because it needed to be done and no one else would do it?	
Cooperative	Do you get along with your co-workers and bosses? Do you always do your part on a team? Can you accept supervision and constructive criticism? Do you volunteer to help?	
Courteous	Do you treat co-workers and customers with respect? Do you listen attentively to others?	

(continued)

(continued)

ADAPTIVE SKILLS CHECKLIST

Adaptive Skill	Behaviors	Rating (1–5)
Dependable	Do you have a good attendance record? Can your supervisor and co-workers count on you when the workload is heavy? Do you follow through on assignments without being checked?	
Dressed Appropriately	Can you adapt your dress style to the style of the business? Do you present a clean and neat appearance?	
Efficient	Do you plan your time well? Do you consciously try to improve your work habits?	
Enthusiastic	Are you interested in your work? Do you inspire others with your own interest?	
Honest	Are you careful with company property and supplies? Do you accept blame for your own mistakes? Do you give praise to others when they do good work?	
Industrious	Are you a self-starter? Do you work steadily on a task until it is done? Do you avoid interruptions?	
Open-Minded	Are you able to accept ideas contrary to your own? Do you adapt well to change?	
Orderly	Do you keep things where they belong? Do you arrange things in a logical way? Are you good with details?	

ADAPTIVE SKILLS CHECKLIST		
Adaptive Skill	Behaviors	Rating (1–5)
Patient	Can you keep your temper? When other people make you angry, do you think before you speak? Are you able to talk to customers calmly, even when you have to explain the same thing over again?	
Persistent	Can you stick to a task even when your enthusiasm and patience are thin? Have you ever accomplished something in spite of great obstacles?	
Punctual	Do you show up for work on time? Do you turn in assignments when they are due?	
Resourceful	Do you see what needs to be done and do it without being told? Do you explore all possible means of solving a problem?	
Tolerant	Can you get along with people of different social, racial, or religious backgrounds? Do you treat all people with respect?	

Functional Skills

The second kind of skills in the skills triangle are called functional skills. These skills are developed through formal education, but also through non-school activities such as scouting and 4-H. Functional skills such as "repairing equipment," "organizing events," and "serving customers" are often learned through extracurricular activities and part-time jobs rather than through formal education. They are not tied to a particular job title, activity, or assignment. They are general skills that can be applied to a variety of life and employment tasks later on.

Functional skills are broad-based, generic skills working with people, data and things. "Analyze information," "set up equipment," "supervise people," "teach others," "negotiate," "persuade," "operate machinery," and "solve problems" are examples of functional skills. "Read," "write," and "solve math problems" are some of the functional skills young people begin to develop in elementary school and continue to develop in high school and in college. Others include "research information," "organize ideas," and "speak before groups." In the job market, people apply their functional skills to a variety of specific work tasks depending on the requirements of the job. Functional skills are "transferable" from one job to the next. They are "portable."

Specific-Content Skills

At the top of the skills pyramid are specific-content skills. These are skills you tend to see in the foreground when you think of someone's skills.

"Reviewing auto insurance claims," "diagnosing cancer," "setting up an IV drip," "testing soil quality," "setting numerical controls for an auto-assembly line," "selling cruises," and "writing binding legal contracts" are all examples of specific content skills. They are the actual job duties an employee is paid money to perform.

Behind each of the specific contents skills lies a broader set of functional and adaptive skills that enable the person to perform the specific content skills of the job. Identifying your child's current set of adaptive and functional skills will help you guide your child with career planning.

Right now your child has a backpack full of skills. It may not contain many specific content skills, but it does contain many adaptive and functional skills. The easiest way to identify the contents of your child's backpack is to ask, "What is my child good at?"

Chances are you will say things like "Joe is a hard worker," "Lisa is really good at math," or "Lenny never knew a stranger." You may use words such as "creative," "gets along with everyone," "kind to others," and "a great writer" to describe your child. These are all adaptive and functional skills. These are your child's strengths. Using the Skills Brainstorming Exercise, you can lead with your child's strengths. You can begin to think about your child's skills in relation to his interests and come up with job titles for career exploration. This is another approach to career planning.

Skills Brainstorming Exercise		
Skills	**Subjects/Activities**	**Potential Job Titles**

Skills Examples:

Build, Repair, Fix, Work Outdoors, Use Tools, Operate Machinery
Research, Analyze, Investigate, Experiment, Solve Math Problems, Solve Scientific Problems
Draw, Paint, Act, Compose, Write, Design
Help, Teach, Train, Care for Others, Listen, Explain
Manage, Sell, Motivate, Speak Before Groups, Persuade, Lead
Organize, Track, Enter Data, Verify

One thing this exercise illustrates is the importance of adaptive and functional skills to career success. It also suggests that the choice of college major is not the deciding factor in success on many jobs.

For many jobs, the college major does not determine marketability. Work experience—both paid and unpaid—while in college, along with a degree in any one of a number of college majors, will determine your child's marketability upon graduation.

Given this fact, how can you help your child de-stress about choosing a college major? How can you reduce the cost of frequent college major changes?

Parent Tip 11

If you have ever been a hiring manager for an organization, you know the value of adaptive skills in the job search. Most people who are fired "for cause" are fired for having poor adaptive skills. Most people who are promoted in a company demonstrate the adaptive skills valued by the employer.

As a parent, it is easy to get so focused on your child's academic skills that you lose sight of her other strengths. Your child's adaptive skills will be as important as her grades to her long-term career success.

(continued)

(continued)

Adaptive skills are behaviors that must be learned and practiced. Name and affirm your child's adaptive skills in everyday life. Think about how you can help your child develop better adaptive skills.

Parent Tip 12

When you went to work after high school or college, chances are jobs were compartmentalized by skills. An employee was hired primarily to work with people, work with data, or work with things. A social worker didn't have to use mechanical equipment. A mechanic didn't have to have excellent people skills. An insurance underwriter didn't have to work extensively with people or with things.

Technology has changed all that. Every social worker now has to use computers (things) to file extensive paperwork (data) before receiving insurance payments for services. Every furnace repair technician now has to train customers (people) how to use electronic furnace controls. Every graphic designer has to use sophisticated computer software to create advertising materials. Part of the stress on workers in the last 25 years has been learning to use skills that were not originally part of the job description—using computers to process customer orders, analyzing statistical data to write program grants, and calibrating sophisticated computer controls to run an assembly line.

Jobs are no longer solely about people, data, or things. Few well-paying jobs today will reward an employee who has skills in only one skill silo. Having a solid background in the STEM subjects of science, technology, engineering, and math is important for all students, not just for students going into math, science, and engineering careers.

Parent Tip 13

Parents and teachers often tell young people to "do something you love." A variation on this theme is "find your passion." But as advice goes, this is pretty vague. What does "do something you love" mean in real life?

If you ask a highly successful life-insurance salesperson, "Why do you love your job?" chances are the answer won't be "Because I have always loved life-insurance products."

The answer will be something like, "I love building relationships and helping people solve problems. I like being my own boss. I like having control over my income potential based on how hard I work and how good I am at my job."

Talk to the people you know who love their jobs. You will find that they feel that way for a variety of reasons, only one of which is the subject matter of the job. For most adults, using skills they enjoy in a work environment that satisfies their values is what makes a job something they love. Informational interviews will help your child begin to understand this.

CHAPTER 6

Choosing a College Major

Many young people experience great anxiety about choosing a college major. This is because they confuse choosing a major with choosing a first career. For many students, choosing a major becomes a once and for all life-or-death decision that will determine career happiness for the rest of their lives. Who wouldn't be ambivalent faced with such a choice? Who wouldn't want to put it off as long as possible?

Simplifying the Process

Here is an activity that will help you and your child de-stress about choosing a major.

Take the list of college majors at the school your child is attending. Sort it into two lists.

In the first list, write down any major that can be converted directly into a job title at the bachelor's degree level. (If you are unsure about the level of education needed for a job, look it up in the *Occupational Outlook Handbook.*)

List I

Major	Job Title
Accounting	Accountant
Interior Design	Interior Designer
Engineering	Engineer
Athletic Training	Athletic Trainer

(continued)

(continued)

Major	Job Title
Graphic Design	Graphic Designer
Nursing	Nurse
Medical Technology	Medical Technologist
Social Work	Social Worker
Elementary Education	Elementary Teacher

In the second list, write down all the other majors.

List II	
Major	
Communications Studies	
English	
History	
Theatre	
Criminal Justice	
Business	
Women's Studies	
Psychology	
Political Science	
Economics	
Biology	
Chemistry	

In the first list, you have majors that give your child specific content skills (see Chapter 5) as part of the upper-division coursework required for an undergraduate degree.

The second list contains majors that give your child functional skills as part of the major, but they do not give your child career-specific skills.

One kind of major is not better or worse than another, but each requires a different career-planning strategy to ensure that the major translates into a successful entry-level career.

Some majors, such as engineering, accounting, education, and interior design, teach your child specific-content skills as part of the upper-division, or "major," coursework. This means the courses your child takes during his junior and senior years in college will teach him the "tools of the trade." The upper-division classes in a specific-content major teach your child the skills he will need to be considered for employment in an entry-level job in a particular field upon graduation.

Other majors, such as English, history, economics, and psychology, do not teach your child specific-content skills at the bachelor's degree level. These undergraduate majors develop broad-based functional skills through a major field of study. They do not prepare your child for a specific entry-level job upon graduation.

The majors in List II develop functional or transferable skills. They give your child general skills that he can "transfer" or apply to a variety of work settings. But it is up to your child to figure out where in the economy he wants to use his functional skills upon graduation.

Specific-Content Majors

Research for the majors in List I is easy. The major directs your child to the job title. Your child can read about the job on the Internet and conduct informational interviews with several people working in the field, as outlined in Chapters 3 and 4.

For specific-content majors, the degree plan is the career plan. Grades, work experience, and participation in professional clubs will enhance the marketability of your child's accounting major, but no professional accountant job will be open to him without an accounting degree.

When your child is considering a specific-content major such as accounting, he needs to answer three questions:

- Am I going to like being an accountant?
- Am I capable of and motivated to do the academic work needed to achieve this career goal?
- Is there a good job market for this career?

Your child can answer these questions by conducting informational interviews with accountants.

Transferable Skills Majors

Research for careers related to the majors in List II is more complicated. This is because the major does not direct your child to a job title.

For the majors in List II, in addition to selecting a major field to study, your child needs to identify where he wants to apply his functional skills after leaving college. For transferable skills majors, a major field of study is not the same thing as a career field.

Many of the majors in List II are called liberal arts majors. The term "liberal arts" describes a curriculum designed to teach general knowledge and develop intellectual capacity rather than teach professional, vocational, or technical skills. It comes from the Latin word "libera," or "free," and refers to the classical understanding of the purpose of the education given to a free man in ancient times as opposed to the education given to a slave. In modern colleges and universities, the term "liberal arts" refers to the broad-based study of art, literature, science, foreign languages, history, and mathematics. A liberal arts degree such as English, mathematics, or history today is contrasted with a career-oriented or technical degree, such as engineering, business, or education.

Many private colleges in the United States began as small liberal arts colleges. Their mission was to form well-rounded individuals who were prepared to pursue further training for a profession or go back into their communities to contribute to work and civic life. Many students who earned liberal arts degrees in the past knew they were going on to study theology, law, or medicine. In "skills" language, a liberal arts degree gave these students the functional and adaptive skills they would need to train for a specific profession or go home to run the family business.

A liberal arts major at a college or a university today is an area of in-depth study within a liberal arts curriculum. The purpose of a liberal arts major is to impart general knowledge and develop the intellectual capacities and values of a student. It is not to prepare students for a particular career. In addition, all college degrees, even in career-focused majors in the professions, include a block of liberal arts courses. Students usually refer to these courses as "the basics," while professors refer to these as "the general-education core." The goal of a liberal arts education, whether through the general-education core or a full liberal arts major, is to develop an educated individual who can leave college and apply his education to any number of enterprises, both work and volunteer.

The thing to understand is that a liberal arts major does not develop specific job skills at the undergraduate level. It develops non-specific transferable skills. A young adult with a bachelor's degree in psychology or economics is a generalist. He does not have the specific-content skills necessary to be employed as a psychologist or economist upon graduation. To learn the specific-content skills needed for paid employment in those careers, he would have to go to graduate school.

Liberal Arts Major	Job Title	Degree Required
History	Historian	M.A./Ph.D.
Economics	Economist	M.A./Ph.D.
Geology	Geologist	M.A./Ph.D.
Chemistry	Chemist	M.A./Ph.D.
Psychology	Psychologist	M.A./Ph.D.
Biology	Biologist	M.A./Ph.D.

While economist and psychologist are certainly careers for an economics or psychology major to research, less than 5 percent of U.S. jobs require a master's degree or higher. Therefore, most liberal arts majors will not be employed in jobs directly related to their field of study. The majority of liberal arts graduates will take their liberal arts skills into the economy, where they will, hopefully, find something interesting to do. Some of the functional skills of a liberal arts major include the following:

Write

Analyze

Research

Solve quantitative problems

Speak before groups

Design

Synthesize information

Coordinate projects

Listen

Make presentations

Think critically

Use technology to perform these skills

Employers often see science and math majors as having stronger quantitative skills than liberal arts majors, who they consider to have stronger communication skills. But all liberal arts majors have basically the same functional skills in terms of the job market. It is up to the liberal arts student to identify a place in the job market to use his functional skills and focus his skills on a first career. This is the issue behind the question, "What can I do with a major in…?"

Liberal Arts Majors and the Economy

In the '60s and '70s, many liberal arts graduates applied their functional skills in business. Management ranks in the U.S. economy were expanding, and there was an undersupply of college graduates to fill them. The belief that if you just got a bachelor's degree, no matter what the major, you would get a good job was true for many people who graduated from college in the '60s and '70s.

In the '80s and '90s, things began to change. Many factors, including technology, globalization, and rising health-care costs, changed the employment landscape. Many of the management jobs once held by liberal arts graduates were eliminated. Management hierarchies were "flattened," and employees who still had their jobs were encouraged to look laterally or to other companies for additional career challenges rather than look up the promotional ladder for more job satisfaction.

As the economy changed, the job prospects of liberal arts majors changed. Students began to gravitate to career-focused but nonspecific-content majors such as business or criminal justice. Parents often felt these majors were more "practical" than an English or sociology major.

A major in business or criminal justice sounds like it is developing specific-content skills, but it does not prepare a graduate for a specific entry-level career. It directs a student's education to a particular sector of the economy. It does not prepare a student for a specific job title within that sector.

It is up to the student to figure out where within the business or criminal justice field he wants to work and get the necessary work experience while in college to make himself marketable upon graduation.

How can you help your child research the employment options of a liberal arts or business major?

Start by searching the Internet for "careers by college major." This search will direct you to the Web sites of various colleges across the country that have organized major and job titles for students.

Liberal arts graduates end up working in a variety of careers. Have your child use the College Major Exercise to identify some job titles associated with the liberal arts major he is considering. He will need to follow up with Internet research and informational interviews to identify the additional skills and work experience he can get while in college to help him land a job after graduation. The key to the marketability of a liberal arts major is work experience during college.

College Major Exercise

College Major	Potential Job Title	Additional Work Experience/Skills Needed

Consider Andy:

Andy was good at math in high school. Because of this, his high school counselor suggested engineering as a career.

Andy's dad, Pete, liked this idea because he had always wanted to be an engineer. He supported Andy in pursuing an engineering degree. Andy won a "Bright Flight" scholarship to his state's flagship university, joined a fraternity, and began his pre-engineering studies.

Andy had completed an advanced pre-calculus course in high school and was placed into a five-credit-hour Calculus I class in college. This was the first of three five-hour calculus classes Andy would need for an engineering degree. Andy had completed a college composition class and 16 credit hours of German in high school, but had opted out of the advanced-placement American history course. He was now enrolled in American History I in college, along with Calculus I, College Chemistry I, and a first-year College Orientation course.

Andy's American history course was taught by a full-time professor in a large lecture hall with 400 students. As part of the course, Andy was required to participate in a small-group discussion two times a week taught by a graduate teaching assistant in history.

Andy struggled with his Calculus I class but managed to pull off a grade of B. He got an A in his American history class. His professor was an expert in the military history of the Civil War. Andy signed up for another history course taught by this same professor the next semester. He also signed up for Calculus II, Introduction to the Engineering Profession, and College Chemistry II.

Andy was barely able to pull off a C in Calculus II. In addition, he found he had little in common with the pre-engineering majors he met in the introduction to engineering class. An engineering major did not feel like a good fit. At the end of his first year in college, Andy e-mailed his dad that he was changing his major to history.

Pete was disappointed and worried about this news. What was Andy going to do with a history major?

When Andy came home for the summer, Pete sat him down for a talk. He asked Andy to consider a business major. Pete thought it would be more marketable than a history major.

Andy said that he thought the business courses sounded boring. Andy said he had talked to his advisor, who told him it was his life and he should study what he wanted, not what his father wanted. Pete said that was fine, but Andy was going to have to come up with a game plan that included life after college along with having fun while he was still in school.

Pete showed Andy some Web sites about careers and college majors. He asked Andy to spend some time in the next month looking at this information, identifying some job titles, and doing some Internet research on the jobs he identified. Pete said he wanted to have another conversation about career issues before Andy left for college in the fall.

A few weeks later, Andy brought up the idea of urban planning as a career. This job title had appeared on several Web sites about careers for history majors. It sounded like something Andy would like. He asked his dad if he knew anyone he could talk to about this field.

Pete thought about his own network and realized he knew a woman through work whose husband worked at City Hall in some sort of strategic-planning position. He talked to his co-worker about his son's interest, and she arranged for Andy to meet with her husband.

Andy went down to City Hall and spent an afternoon with people working in various aspects of city planning and development. They told him he would need a master's degree in urban planning to advance, but some entry-level positions were available to bachelor's degree holders. Andy was encouraged to take some Geographic Information Systems (GIS) courses at the local community college along with his history degree and was invited to apply for an internship in the department the next summer.

Andy was on track to use his math and analytical skills in a career other than engineering. His work experience in college, along with his specialized skills in GIS, would make him marketable for an entry-level position in his chosen field. By supporting his son in a positive way, Pete avoided a relationship-bruising battle with Andy over choice of college major and at the same time was pleased with the end results.

Key Points in Choosing a College Major

Here are the basics that you, as a parent, need to teach your college student about how degrees and majors relate to the job market:

- There are many reasons why people go to college and many benefits of a college education. In the job market, a college degree is a credential. It demonstrates or proves to an employer that you have the skills to do the things the employer wants done.
- Different majors give you different skills in the job market. Some majors give you specific-content skills as part of your major. Others give you broad-based functional skills. One kind of major is not better than another, but each requires a different career-planning strategy on your part if you want to find a job after graduation.
- Some majors, like engineering, accounting, education, and interior design, teach you specific-content skills. This means that in your junior- and senior-level courses, you learn the "tools of the trade."

Your upper-division classes in a specific-content major teach you the skills you need to be considered for employment in an entry-level job in that field upon graduation.

- Other majors, like English, history, economics, and psychology, do not give you specific-content skills. They give you broad-based functional skills that you develop through a major field of study. In resume-writing language, liberal arts majors give you "transferable" skills.
- A liberal arts field of study is not the same thing as a career field. If you choose a liberal arts major, you don't have a career field. You have a field of study. It's up to you to figure out where you want to use your skills in the economy after you graduate from college. Liberal arts majors have two, rather than one, decisions to make. They need to decide what subject to major in and where they want to use their functional skills in the job market.
- A specific-content major is preparation for a particular job title. It is up to you to find out the demand for those jobs. Just because there is a specific-content major in a field doesn't mean there are a lot of jobs in the field. Engineering, accounting, athletic training, and broadcast journalism are all specific-content majors. Each prepares you for a particular career. Each of these careers, however, has a very different profile when it comes to job openings, starting salary, and the number of workers who are self-employed. It is up to you to find this information out.
- The demand for liberal arts graduates has always been relative to the economy at the time. In the past 20 years, many management jobs that once employed liberal arts generalists have been eliminated. If you choose a liberal arts major today, you need to start looking while you are in college to identify where you want to work upon graduation. You need to network, conduct informational interviews, and get relevant work experience. You cannot assume a good job will be waiting for you just because you have a college degree. The management hierarchies that absorbed your parents have been flattened. At the same time, there are more college graduates than ever before.
- Graduate school is another way people acquire specific-content skills. But jobs that require a master's, doctorate, or first professional degree—such as psychologist, biologist, or lawyer—are subject to the same laws of supply and demand as any other job. If you plan to go to graduate school, you need to research the job outlook for the career you want enter.

The College Majors Tips Sheet summarizes these ideas.

COLLEGE MAJORS TIPS SHEET

Examples:

Specific-Content Skills Majors	Functional Skills Majors
Accounting	Psychology
Engineering	Economics
Athletic Training	English
Elementary Education	Biology
Interior Design	Communication
Construction Management	Mathematics
Pharmacy	History

"In-Between" Majors
Business
Criminal Justice
Animal Technology
Journalism
Environmental Studies

- Majors that teach you specific-content skills prepare you for a particular job title in the economy.

  Research these majors by conducting informational interviews and doing job shadows to make sure you will like doing the job and there is a demand for the job in the economy.

- Majors that give you functional skills prepare you to do a variety of general functions in a wide range of industries and careers. It is up to you to figure out where in the economy you want to apply your functional skills after graduation.

  Research these majors by doing an Internet search for "careers by college majors." Get work experience while you are in college to shape a career path after graduation.

(continued)

(continued)

- Majors that give you in-between skills teach you about a particular sector of the economy, but they do not prepare you for a particular job title within that sector.

  Research these majors by talking to someone currently working in the field to identify job titles in that sector of the economy. Get work experience while you are in college to shape your career path after graduation.

Choosing a major is one criterion to use in selecting a college. What are some other things to consider in deciding where your child should go to school?

Parent Tip 14

Just because there is a major in a field doesn't mean there are a lot of jobs in the field. Jobs can be "high density" or "low density." Skills can be in high demand or low demand. A software engineering major and an interior design major both have specific-content skills, but their skills have different values in the labor market. These majors have different profiles when it comes to jobs available and compensation and benefits associated with those jobs.

Your child needs to research the job market for a major before, not after, choosing a specific-content major. Make sure your child's expectations for the marketability of his major are grounded in the realities of the job market.

Parent Tip 15

Make sure your child conducts informational interviews with people who are earning a living working in a field full time, not just with professors in the corresponding academic department or college representatives.

While college professors and other college personnel can be excellent resources about careers, particularly if they are working in the field in addition to teaching, there is no substitute for talking to people working full time in the field. Your child needs to find out exactly how the major is playing out in today's job market. Have your child spend time on the job (job shadowing) with someone who is an engineer, elementary school teacher, or interior designer to get an accurate assessment of the job market and to make sure the job is something she will enjoy.

Parent Tip 16

One reason most people don't find themselves, career-wise, in college is because college is not the best place to find your first career. Beyond a relatively short list of college majors that lead directly to high-paying jobs, most jobs in the economy have a much more indirect connection to a college major.

Most young people need to spend time looking in the workplace to find out where they belong, rather than switching from major to major to find career direction. The standard advice to college freshmen to keep all options open and sample a variety of courses to identify a career path simply normalizes indecision and racks up family college costs.

Unless you have unlimited funds to pay for college, you need to encourage your child to select a major and complete it. At the same time, you need to support your child in researching areas of the economy where she might find interesting work to do after graduation. You need to help her get relevant work experience while in college to enhance her marketability upon graduation.

Parent Tip 17

If your child wants to major in history and you want him to major in business, let him major in history.

Many parents get confused by "middle-ground" majors such as business and criminal justice. They feel these majors offer more concrete skills and are, therefore, more marketable than liberal arts majors such as English and sociology.

But most jobs require both education and work experience for employment. For many jobs, work experience trumps college major.

If your child has ruled out the specific-content majors at his college, it doesn't really matter, jobwise, what major your child selects. This is because his work experience—paid employment, internships, and volunteer positions—will determine his career path after college, not his college major. Rather than pressure a liberal arts–oriented student to choose a major in business, encourage him to pick a major he will enjoy and go for it.

At the same time, help him look for interesting jobs to do so that he can gain work experience while in college that will make him marketable upon graduation.

Parent Tip 18

Many parents complain about the "bad advising" their child received in college. These parents (and many college graduates) have hard feelings about all the money "bad advising" cost them.

In reality, the term "advising" is an easy target for parental frustration because it means so many things to different people. Advising functions are performed by a variety of college personnel in a variety of college offices. Identify the various offices at the college that provide "advising" so you can help your child get the help he needs when he needs it.

At parent orientation, get clear in your own mind which office on campus performs the following functions and find out what those offices are called at your child's particular institution, including

- Academic-advising services to help your child select and schedule classes each semester.
- Career-counseling services to help your child decide on a major and identify an initial career path.
- Career-placement services to help your child find internships and get work experience while in college.
- Career-planning services to help your child write a resume, interview effectively, and network to find a job after college.
- Personal-counseling services to help your child cope with the stress of college life.

All of these functions get lumped together in students' minds as "advising." Many students fault their "advising" when in reality it is their own lack of career planning that is the problem. The best advisor in the world can't guarantee all your child's courses will apply to his degree if your child is undecided between journalism and engineering. You, as a parent, need to get clear as to who provides what service on campus so you can encourage your child to seek out the appropriate resources at each step of the way.

Parent Tip 19

Admission to a college or university does not guarantee admission to a particular major. Some majors have higher GPA requirements and stricter rules about prerequisite courses than other majors. In addition, some majors have "gateway" courses such as business calculus that may only be offered at certain times of the academic year. If your child is off track for the gateway course, this can add another year to college costs.

It will be very difficult for your child to keep all options open and still complete the prerequisite requirements for the major she finally selects. Encourage your child to take courses that she is interested in but that will also meet the requirements for the various majors she is considering. Encourage her to meet every semester with an academic advisor and get help in the career center with choosing a major.

Parent Tip 20

One of many debates going on within higher education today is whether college is supposed to be about "education" or "training."

The "college is about education" position is that the purpose of higher education is to develop critical-thinking skills in students and shape student values. It is not to prepare students for jobs after graduation. The "college is about training" position is that higher education needs to produce people who can contribute to the economy after they get out of school. Many land-grant universities were established to fulfill this mission.

In the '60s and '70s, the "education" versus "training" argument was irrelevant to many students and their parents because students with a general liberal arts education were graduating from college and finding good jobs with companies and organizations willing to train them to do something in the economy. Many U.S. businesses had healthy training budgets and were structurally set up to bring on college graduates and train them to do various functions within their organizations. These college graduates were then ready to move up the ladder to better jobs with better pay.

Times have changed. With many U.S. companies being sold to larger companies, and as outsourcing shifts many jobs formerly done in-house to smaller, more specialized firms, liberal arts graduates need to be more resourceful in identifying places to work and more effective in marketing their transferable skills to employers. Liberal arts graduates need to have a very clear answer to the question, "Why should an employer hire me?"

Parent Tip 21

In the aftermath of the latest recession, less than half of U.S. recent college graduates age 25 and under were working in jobs that required a college degree. Studies show that college graduates who begin their career in lower-paying jobs below their education level often take seven to nine years to catch up with the earnings of fellow graduates who start out at jobs that require a college degree. The experience of recent college graduates working outside their field of education, training, and choice has been dubbed "mal-employment" in the popular media. In reality, this is "underemployment." It is a problem not only for new college graduates but for many other people who hold college degrees as well. According to the BLS, in 2008 more than 6.3 million U.S. workers with bachelor's degrees or higher were working in jobs that required only short-term on-the-job training. Jobs in this category are defined as ones in which "...the skills needed to be fully qualified in the occupation can be acquired during a short demonstration of job duties or during one month or less of on-the-job experience or instruction." The number of workers in this short-term on-the-job training category in 2008 included 5,264,200 people with bachelor's degrees, 862,900 people with master's degrees, and 206,100 people with doctoral or professional degrees. In addition, another 3,789,200 people with associate degrees were working in jobs requiring only short-term OJT.

This is important information for any parent planning on a child using student loans to pay for college. What do you expect your child's marketability to be upon graduation from college? How will that impact your child's ability to pay off his or her student loans?

The fact is that college X will cost approximately the same amount whether your child is a political science major, a chemical engineering major, or an athletic training major. Graduates in each of these disciplines will experience a different demand for their skills when they enter the job market.

In terms of the job market, it is important to look beyond the level of the degree, whether associate, bachelor's, master's, or Ph.D., to the skills represented by a degree in a particular discipline and the demand for those skills in the labor market. Borrow money to pay for college accordingly.

Parent Tip 22

There is no official government definition of a "green" job, but students who are interested in greening the planet might consider engineering as a career. Many of the well-paying jobs improving the environment require the scientific and technical background of an engineering degree. Students who are interested in green jobs can major in a traditional area of engineering, such as civil, chemical, electrical, or mechanical, and focus on a green emphasis at the graduate level.

If your child does not have the math or physics skills necessary to become an engineer, he can research technician-level jobs in the energy industry. Many of the current jobs in today's electric, gas, oil, and water industry occupations may be converting to green jobs in the future. Many workers will shift their current transferable and specific job skills to jobs in renewable energy production, such as wind or solar power and biofuel production. While traditional energy jobs are not projected to grow over the next 10 years, thousands of these well-paying technician-level jobs will open up as baby boomers retire. The educational paths to these jobs include on-the-job training, technical training at a career center or community college, or a bachelor's degree in engineering technology.

Parent Tip 23

Your child can choose a career first and then choose a major or choose a major first and then choose an initial career path. One strategy isn't better than the other, but each requires homework outside of class. As tempting as it may be for your child to procrastinate on career and major research, it is in his best interest to engage in the career-planning process earlier rather than later. Each additional year of college at a public university for an in-state student will cost between $8,000 and $10,000 in tuition, books, and fees. This does not include the cost of room and board for each additional year of college.

Parent Tip 24

Any student interested in the arts as a college major will, at some point, have to look at the issue of whether to pursue art as a vocation or avocation. A student in the arts must ask, "What is the likelihood that I will be able to make a living with my art?"

Paid employment in the arts is very competitive. Only one percent of all jobs are in the arts, and employment often depends more on talent and connections than academic degree. Every student interested in the arts should be encouraged to follow her passion, but also develop a Plan B as a way to make a living while she continues with her art.

There are also non-performance careers that may offer your child both fulfillment and the opportunity to use her major. For example, someone who has

(continued)

(continued)

studied painting and sculpture may seek employment in a museum's preservation department. Securing many of the non-performance jobs can still be very competitive.

Parent Tip 25

After years of shuttling a child between dance, drama, and music lessons, parents often seem surprised when their child announces a desire to major in the arts in college. At this point, parent economic concerns kick in, and they ask, "How are you going to support yourself with a degree in theatre?"

This is where you, as a parent, need to back off and let your child figure this out himself. You need to honor, respect, and celebrate your child's artistic gifts. If your child truly has the passion and talent to pursue a career in the arts, your rational economic concerns will not stop him.

At the same time, you need to make sure he has realistic expectations about what his economic situation will be after college when he is trying to establish himself in an artistic career. This is especially important if he will be responsible for paying off student loans.

Informational interviews with other artists will help your child clarify his expectations. Your child needs to be honest about the job market he will face and understand that if he is not able to earn a living in the arts, he still has many other transferable skills that he can use in other jobs. He can continue to enjoy and explore his art in his non-work time. This is career/life balance.

CHAPTER 7

Going Away vs. Staying at Home

One year of room and board at a residential college currently costs between $7,000 and $15,000, depending on the school. This room and board amount, along with personal and transportation expenses over and above those expenses your child would incur living at home, is what you and your child will be paying for "the college experience."

The "college experience" is shorthand for the constellation of experiences a young adult will have living away from home for the first time, out from under the watchful eyes of parents. In skills language, a positive college experience develops important adaptive and functional skills, including time management, cooperation, and budgeting. By living with diverse personalities in the close confines of a residence hall; balancing multiple demands on time that include study, social, and work obligations; navigating the bureaucracy of higher education; adjusting to increased academic rigor and competition; and staying physically and emotionally fit through it all, your child will emerge from the college experience a stronger, more independent young adult, but one who has also had a good time along the way.

At least, this is what you are hoping will happen.

Outcomes are not always as good. Students who pay more attention to social rather than study commitments can "party out" of college, coming home with 20 college credits and $20,000 in debt. Academically strong students can get caught up in the social scene and put scholarships in jeopardy by earning a lower-than-expected grade point average their freshman year.

Is Your Child Ready to Go Away to School?

How do you know if your child is ready to go away to college?

There are three things to consider in assessing your child's readiness to go away to college: academic preparedness, social/emotional preparedness, and financial preparedness.

Academic Preparedness

Academic preparedness is the easiest to determine. What are your child's current skill levels in writing, reading, and math? Find this by having your child take the ACT test fall or spring of junior year or by having your child go to the local community college and take the COMPASS test. You can then compare your child's ACT or COMPASS scores to ACT's College Readiness Benchmarks.

The ACT College Readiness Benchmarks are the ACT test scores required for students to have a high probability of success in the credit-bearing (not remedial) college courses many students typically take in their first year of college. These first-year courses include English composition, social science courses such as American history and psychology, biology, and college algebra. ACT has done extensive research on college readiness. The benchmark numbers are the minimum ACT or COMPASS scores that students would need to achieve in order to have a 50 percent chance of earning a grade of B or better or a 75 percent chance of earning a C or better in the corresponding college courses. The ACT looks at English, reading, math, and science skills, while the COMPASS looks at English, reading, and math. Do an Internet search for "ACT college readiness benchmarks" to see a chart of benchmark scores.

Another aspect of academic success in college is what high school counselors call the ability to "play school." This is your child's ability to adapt to the norms and culture of the institution, whether high school or college, in order to achieve academic goals. The ability to "play school" includes doing homework outside of class, turning in assignments on time, meeting teacher expectations, engaging in classroom discussions constructively, asking questions, getting along with teachers, using the library and online resources, managing time, and meeting multiple project deadlines. All of these behaviors shape the "habits of mind" needed for success in college. How well does your child "play school" in high school? How well do you think she will "play school" in college?

One indicator is how much time your child is spending on homework outside class during her junior and senior year in high school. Students who attend college will be expected to spend at least two hours per week of outside study time for each credit hour of class. A student who is taking 15 college credit hours will need to budget at least 30 outside study hours each week to be successful in those classes. This amount of independent study can be a shock for an academically strong student attending college for the first time. It can be a time-management disaster for a student who is not accustomed to doing any homework at all.

Another indicator of your child's academic readiness for college is her success in high school math. Almost all bachelor's degrees require college algebra or another course in quantitative reasoning. To avoid taking remedial math courses in college and the corresponding delay in completing a degree, your child should take as much math as possible in high school, including a math course senior year. Studies show that one year of high school math beyond algebra II can increase your child's chances of completing a bachelor's degree by 50 percent.

A third indicator of your child's readiness for college is how well she can write. College students are expected to produce numerous short papers, as well as longer research papers, in a variety of classes, not just in English classes. Going into college, your child will be expected to read unfamiliar material, analyze it, and respond critically in writing. She will be expected to write quickly and concisely in response to essay test questions. How well does your child write? Has she written a research paper in high school in which she has referenced multiple sources using a standardized writing style guide? Your child should be comfortable and confident in her writing skills when she goes to college in order to be successful.

Social/Emotional Preparedness

Social/emotional preparedness is the second factor you need to look at in assessing your child's readiness for college.

This is a more subjective matter than academic preparedness. It involves your child's resilience and resourcefulness and her ability to set personal boundaries and make good choices in a new, unregulated environment. It is about how sensible, practical, and organized your child is and how easy or hard it is for her to make new friends, ask for help, and be open to new interests.

College, and especially the transition to college freshman year, is stressful. Many parents romanticize their own college experience as a sort of idyllic break between childhood and adult responsibilities. But college was stressful back when you were in school, and it is stressful for young people today. More students who are academically underprepared for college are attending college today. These students, along with their more academically prepared counterparts, are taking on much more debt than students 20 years ago to pay for college. Young people experience stressors that didn't exist when you were in school. Errors of judgment in the party scene that would have caused you private remorse 20 years ago can be recorded on a cell phone and publicly shared on the Internet. Going away to college means leaving a support system behind and creating a new one. How well do you think your child will handle this challenge?

Step back and think about your child. What are her personal strengths and weaknesses? As you imagine her in a new college environment, how well do you think she will do making new friends? Will she have a support system already in place in terms of friends from home attending the same college? Will these friends be a positive or negative influence? Is she likely to join campus groups of students who share similar interests? Will she be joining a sorority and have a new support system there? How well do you think she will handle situations in which alcohol is involved? Does she have a track record of setting healthy personal boundaries in unregulated social situations? Do you anticipate your child being homesick or "friend-sick" in that she will be emotionally focused on family and friends in other locations and not fully engaged in her new environment?

These are all things to consider in making the decision about where to send your child to school.

Financial Preparedness

Finally, there is financial preparedness. This goes beyond having your child develop a budget for living expenses while away at school. Financial preparedness means both you and your child are on the same page about the financial implications of college choice. It means that you both clearly understand how your family will be paying for college.

Financial preparedness means getting clear in your own mind where you stand on the issue of paying for college. Is it your expectation that you will pay for any college, regardless of the cost? Does your child have the same expectation? Can your child go anywhere she wants, as long as she can get admitted? This is the "college first" approach, in which a student selects the college and the parents figure out how to pay for it. Is this the way you see it? If this is the way your child sees it, are you two in agreement?

If you are not going to be able to pay for college, or if you will not be able to pay the full amount, do you expect your child to borrow money for college? If so, how much debt are you comfortable with your child taking on to pay for college? Is the message you are communicating to your child that no amount of money is too great to borrow to go to certain schools? Is this the message your child is getting from family, friends, counselors, teachers, and college recruiters? If so, does your child understand the long-term implications of the debt she will be taking on?

Because college recruiters often communicate with students in the high school before parents are involved, and because recruiters often frame the decision about where to go to college as a "college first" decision, it is important to examine your beliefs around college choice and communicate them clearly to your child before you both get swept up in the emotion of the college admissions process.

You and your child will experience heavy marketing around choosing a college. As the pool of traditional-age students grows smaller in the next few years, there will be more and more recruiting pressure on your child to consider different schools. You need to be clear about where you stand. Talk with your child about how the decision about college will be made in your family. Will the decision be your child's alone? Will it be your decision? Will it be a joint decision, based on the overall financial situation of the family as well as your child's best interest, both academically and financially? This is the "cost first" approach. How much can you afford to pay for college? Given what you can afford, which colleges are the best fit for your child?

The College Fit worksheet will help you organize your thoughts around college fit. Think about your child's academic, social, and financial preparedness for college. Then identify the corresponding information about the colleges your child is considering. This will give you more data upon which you and your child can base the college decision.

	College Fit	
Academic Fit	**Social/Emotional Fit**	**Financial Fit**
Average ACT/SAT; degrees and majors; competitiveness; rankings; graduation rate; class size; education level of instructors; academic pressure; libraries and labs; graduation rate/time; accreditation.	*Size; location; distance from home; public or private; rural or urban setting; housing; sports; religious affiliation; ethnic diversity; facilities; amenities; clubs; fraternities/ sororities; activities/events.*	*Cost of attendance; out-of-pocket expense; scholarships and grants; amount needed to borrow; work-study/ part time jobs; internships; transportation costs.*

A student who is strong both academically and socially and who has unlimited financial resources might be encouraged to go anywhere. A student who is strong academically but socially and emotionally tentative might be encouraged to look at schools closer to home. A college that is a two- to three-hour drive home for the student to recharge and refocus might be a better fit than a college with a six-hour plane flight between school and home. An academically strong student with good social skills but limited financial resources might look for schools providing the best scholarship offers, keeping in mind the need to limit student loans to cover transportation costs and living expenses. A student with good social skills but weak academic skills who has unlimited financial resources might look for a private college that offers a strong academic support program to help her build her skills to the college level and go on to finish a college degree. An academically weak student who is also socially weak, even with unlimited resources, might be wise to attend college close to home until she has demonstrated she is capable of college-level work.

There is no "one size fits all" way to choose a college and no one "right" college for every student. The transition to college is a major developmental milestone, and not all students are at the same developmental stage when they graduate from high school. College choice should be made accordingly.

Whatever decision you and your child make, you will have to come up with the money to pay for it. Is there a way to identify the true cost of college before a child enrolls?

Parent Tip 26

Grade inflation is the practice of giving higher grades for academic work than the work merits.

There are many pressures on high school teachers to reduce standards. Pressure comes from a variety of sources, including parents, school administrators, politicians, and students themselves. If grade inflation is going on at your high school, it will distort your view of your child's college readiness.

Seek out more objective data. In assessing college readiness, have your child take a standardized test like the ACT or COMPASS to get a broader picture of his or her skills. Given the amount of money you will be paying for college, make sure you have good data upon which to base your college decision.

Parent Tip 27

Presumably, if your child makes good grades on standardized tests like the ACT and SAT, she has learned to "play school" effectively. But this is not always the case. A student may earn good test scores on standardized tests while exerting very little effort in high school. The ability to test well without studying will not be enough to sustain your child academically at the college level.

Your child will need to have strong study skills outside of class in order to be successful in college-level work. A student with high standardized test scores but poor study skills will face extra challenges freshman year.

Parent Tip 28

A good way to get ahead of the game when it comes to time management in college is to sit down with your child, once he has gone through new student orientation and is enrolled in classes, and have him map out a weekly planning grid like the one that follows this tip.

First, have him write in his weekly class schedule. Then have him mark out the times he will be working.

(continued)

(continued)

Next, have him mark out times for personal care, including meals and exercise. Finally, have him calculate his needed study time for the credit hours he is taking, applying the two for one rule: two hours of study for each hour in class. Ask him to identify where on the planning grid he might have time to study. When could he study and where might he do so? If the residence hall is too noisy, where are some other places on campus that might be more conducive to study?

Having a student create a weekly time log is often an eye-opener. It gives the student a visual picture of where he is spending his time and an opportunity to regroup if his time management plan is not producing the results he wants in college.

Weekly Planning Grid

Time	Monday	Tuesday	Wednesday	Thursday	Friday	Saturday	Sunday
6:00 AM							
7:00							
8:00							
9:00							
10:00							
11:00							
12:00 N							
1:00 PM							
2:00							
3:00							
4:00							
5:00							

Weekly Planning Grid (continued)

Time	Monday	Tuesday	Wednesday	Thursday	Friday	Saturday	Sunday
6:00							
7:00							
8:00							
9:00							
10:00							
11:00							
12:00 AM							
1:00							
2:00							
3:00							
4:00							
5:00							

Parent Tip 29

If your child scores into remedial courses in college, this is a red flag about his readiness to go away to school. Your child is already behind the pack going out of the starting gate.

You need to identify your child's academic weaknesses while he is in high school and seek out academic support. It is unrealistic to expect a student who has not learned good study strategies in high school to suddenly turn around and demonstrate good study skills in college when all parental structure has been removed.

After your child has taken the ACT or COMPASS test as a junior, set up a meeting with your high school counselor. Map out a game plan of classes and support services for senior year that will help your child build his skills to the college level.

Parent Tip 30

To help your child with the social/emotional transition to college, have a debriefing session with your child after she attends freshman orientation. Using a map of campus, have your child show you the following places:

- The student health center.
- The fitness center, bike trail, or jogging path she can use to keep up an exercise routine.
- The college library.
- The location of the academic support services for writing, math, and course-specific tutoring.
- The counseling center where she can go for help.

Parent Tip 31

In dealing with the financial-aid process and other administrative matters, you have a choice to make. You can choose to do everything for your child yourself or you can teach your child how to navigate the college bureaucracy on her own.

Most parents who encourage their child to go away to college do so because they believe that their child will learn many things outside the classroom. In skills language, many parents think that by living communally in a residence hall, managing her own free time, socializing with new people, and managing money, their child will gain important adaptive and functional skills that will benefit her throughout life.

But some of the most critical life skills learned outside the classroom involve navigating the bureaucracy of higher education. If you do this work yourself, you deny your child the opportunity to learn important skills.

The following are some functional skills you can teach your child through interactions with the bureaucracy of higher education.

- How to use complex software to transact personal business.
- How to communicate effectively using e-mail.
- How to communicate verbally to get your needs met.
- How to read the fine print before you sign anything.
- How to budget.
- How to think through the implications of borrowing money before you do so.

Here are some of the adaptive skills you can teach your child through interactions with the bureaucracy of higher education:

- Responsibility
- Courtesy
- Accuracy
- Attention to detail

If you do all your child's college administrative transactions for her, you are sabotaging her long-term growth and development. While it is always easier in the short run to do the job yourself, it is not in the best long-term interest of your child for you to do so.

Parent Tip 32

To teach your child how to manage her own business affairs in college, you will first need to figure the process out yourself. This means getting access to your child's administrative student account.

There are two main kinds of electronic accounts your child will use in college. One is a student account that gives your child access to classroom-management software. The other is a student account that lets your child do administrative business with the college.

You should have access to your child's administrative account. You should not have access to your child's classroom account.

Classroom-management software allows your child to perform classroom-related functions such as turning in assignments electronically, communicating with instructors about classes, checking grades as the semester progresses, accessing supplemental course materials, and so on. Two widely used classroom-management programs are Blackboard and Web CT.

Student-administration software lets your child perform administrative tasks such as enrolling in classes each semester, checking final grades, reviewing transcripts, paying for college, checking the status of financial aid, and communicating with college personnel about these functions. Student administration software often has a college-specific label like "My State U."

You have no business in your child's classroom-management account. This is like sitting beside your child in the classroom. You must let your child sink or swim on

(continued)

(continued)

her own academically in college. You can direct her to resources on campus that will help her if she tells you she is struggling, but you should not be monitoring the day-to-day interactions of her classes.

On the other hand, you should get access to your child's administrative account for several reasons:

- You are paying for college.
- It may be the only way you will be able to see your child's final grades.
- It is the only way you will be able to teach your child how to perform key administrative functions herself.

Because of federal privacy laws, your child will have to give you access to her administrative records. In a technological age, this is simple. Ask your child to give you her user ID and password for her student-administrative account. In addition, if your child receives financial aid, have her go to the financial aid office and fill out a consent form letting you, as a parent, talk with financial aid personnel about your child's account.

Parent Tip 33

At each step of the administrative process, it is important for you to ask yourself, "Am I going to do this for my child or am I going to teach my child how to do this herself?"

Things you should do yourself:

- Complete your income tax forms as early as possible each year because all financial aid hinges on parental tax information.
- Complete the FAFSA (Free Application for Federal Student Aid) each year even if you think your family income is too great to qualify for federal need-based aid. Your child probably qualifies for federal non-need-based aid, but to be considered for this money, you must complete the FAFSA.
- Educate yourself as to the important dates: the financial aid deadline, the earliest date to enroll, the date fees are due, the last date to withdraw with a full refund, partial refund dates, and so on.
- Monitor your child's progress meeting administrative deadlines.
- Teach your child how to advocate for herself in dealings with college personnel.
- Have a clear understanding of your own financial situation before you sign on for student loan debt.

Things you should encourage your child to do:

- Log in to her student account on a regular basis.
- Check her student e-mail on a regular basis.
- Schedule and attend all testing, advising, enrollment, and orientation sessions.
- Enroll as early as possible each semester.
- Watch for financial aid deadlines.
- Turn in financial aid paperwork on time, whether in person or online.
- Be nice to the people working in the financial aid office.
- Meet with an academic advisor each semester to verify course selection.
- Go to the career center by the second semester of her freshman year to get help selecting a major.
- Advocate for herself with her instructors.
- Seek out academic support services before there are problems in a class.

Things you and your child need to have an honest discussion about before she goes to college:

- How much money your child will be borrowing.
- Where the financial aid money will be spent.
- A budget for living expenses while in college.
- How any student loans will be repaid.
- The use of student loans to pay for needs rather than wants.
- The implication of failed or dropped classes on financial aid eligibility.
- Who pays for failed or dropped courses.
- The comparative values of financial aid offers and the fact that the biggest scholarship is not always the best deal.
- Your own ability to pay for a particular college.
- The financial impact of losing a scholarship because of poor grades.
- Signing credit card offers, including retail store accounts.
- Who pays any credit card balances.

Parent Tip 34

If you are tempted to get into your child's classroom-management account because you pay the bills, stop and think about it. Put yourself in the instructor's

(continued)

(continued)

shoes. Would you want 30 outside people monitoring and critiquing your work every day?

Perhaps you work in a "this call may be monitored" kind of environment. Perhaps you respond well to that kind of supervisory oversight. But if you don't, think about how it would feel if you had to work that way.

Education is about process as much as course content and grades. It is your child's responsibility to engage in the process. It is your child's responsibility to communicate with her instructor and seek out help when needed. And it is your child's responsibility to accept the consequences if the outcome is not what you or she had expected.

Parent Tip 35

Each year *U.S. News and World Report* publishes a list of college rankings. This report is based on a number of criteria, including the fall-to-fall retention rate for students (how many freshmen come back to the same institution the next year), the graduation rate of students who earn a degree in six years or less, and the average class size.

Here are some additional questions to ask college recruiters as you and your child develop your own list of college rankings:

- What are the top five classes in freshman enrollment?
- What is the withdrawal or failure rate in each of the top five classes (i.e., how many students in these classes earn a grade of D or F or withdraw from the class before the semester is over)?
- What are the top five undergraduate majors at this institution? How many students apply to these majors each year, and how many are accepted?
- What is the average student loan debt of graduates of this institution?
- What percentages of first-year students are enrolled in remedial math, writing, and reading classes?

The answers to these questions will help you evaluate whether an institution will be a good fit for your child.

Parent Tip 36

The "college effect" describes an increase in health-risk behaviors related to alcohol use the first semester in college. Students who formerly abstained from alcohol may begin drinking, and students who have been drinking in high school may escalate their drinking now that they are free from parental control.

It is important not to overreact or underreact to college drinking. Educate yourself on the issue. Many Web sites have excellent resource information on the topic. If you suspect your child is having alcohol problems, insist he go to the college counseling center and get an assessment before going back to school the next semester. Confronting your child in this way could be just the wake-up call he needs to change course before it is too late.

Parent Tip 37

One reason to have your child begin basic career exploration in high school is to reduce stress freshman year.

The first year of college is a huge transition for even the best and the brightest of students. Your child will have enough on his plate meeting the increased academic demands of college while making new friends and enjoying a social life. Career planning is, and should be, on the back burner.

At the same time, when your child chooses his classes for sophomore year, he needs to have a tentative major in mind. This is because certain courses are required sophomore year for entry into a major as a junior. Since sophomore enrollment usually takes place on many campuses during the spring of freshman year, your child will need to have a tentative idea of a college major near the end of freshman year to choose the right classes to be on track to graduate in four years.

Parent Tip 38

One of the many issues within higher education today is the tension between a business model of higher education and an academic model. These conflicting models can exist within the same institution and create confusion for students and parents. When is a college like any other business? When is it not? When is your child a customer and when is he a student?

Enrollment management is a business model of higher education. It is focused on increasing net revenue through marketing and customer service. Students and parents are brought into the institution under a business model. Often families have more than a year of interaction with college personnel before new student orientation begins.

(continued)

(continued)

The traditional professor-student relationship is an academic model. It is focused on student learning and helping students learn through all their experiences, including their mistakes and failures. Students and parents are expected to switch gears and relate to the college in an academic model once the student is accepted into school.

It is helpful to give this matter some thought before you interact with college personnel. It is also helpful for college personnel to give this matter some thought before they interact with you!

Parent Tip 39

One reason to have a conversation with your child sooner rather than later about how your family will decide where a he or she will go to college is the increasing use of electronic communication in college recruiting. Colleges are using social networking resources like Facebook and Twitter to communicate with students. Information is distributed directly to potential students in a way that appeals to teenagers and their criteria for choosing a college. The goal of the recruiting process is to create a large pool of applicants. The more students that apply, the easier it is for the college to select the best mix of students to advance its enrollment management goals.

As a parent, you have no idea how any of the online interactions your child has with recruiters will be used in the enrollment management process. Social networking as a recruitment tool is too new for you to predict how it will impact your child's college decision.

You need to get ahead of the game. Have a conversation with your child about how your family will be making the college decision and the need for caution in sharing too much personal information in social networking exchanges with college reps.

Parent Tip 40

The decision to go away to college or attend college while living at home is not an all-or-nothing decision. A student can live at home for an agreed-upon time and then transfer to another institution.

If this is your family game plan, it is important for your student to work closely with the advising office at both schools to make sure all courses will transfer and that all prerequisite courses for a major are included in the plan of study.

Parent Tip 41

If cost is an issue to you, make sure your high school counselor knows what your priorities are and which colleges you are considering.

Many people, including educators, are unaware of how much of today's financial aid packaging consists of loans rather than grants and scholarships. If this will be an issue for you, make sure those influencing your child understand your position. Giving a young person a college education is a tremendous gift, but so is making sure a young person can start adult life with little or no debt.

Parent Tip 42

If your child has not completed college composition and college algebra courses in high school, he may be required to take a placement test before enrolling for those courses as a college freshman. Some schools use the ACT or SAT tests to place students in first-semester college courses, while others have their own placement tests to determine which courses a student must take.

If your child will be taking a placement test before enrolling, make sure he does some review before taking the test. If your child did not take a math course senior year, it is especially important for him to review math concepts before the placement test so he does not score into remedial courses in college. Have your child go to the public library and check out a study guide to use to refresh his skills in writing, reading, and math before taking any college placement test.

Parent Tip 43

When your child calls from college and talks about a problem he is experiencing, he may be venting or he may need your help. You won't know until you listen. Rather than jump into action to fix the problem, say something like, "Tell me what you've done already to solve the problem." By listening carefully and letting your child brainstorm solutions to his own difficulties, you will be teaching problem-solving and self-advocacy skills rather than taking the problem away from your child and fixing it yourself.

Parent Tip 44

The easiest way to determine if you are over the top on any of your parental interventions is to ask yourself, "Would I want to work with my child if this behavior was going on?"

If your child were working in the office cubicle next to yours and assigned to your project team, how would you react if

- His mother called his supervisor to challenge his performance review?
- His dad had online access to your team discussion board and project timelines?
- His mother rewrote his monthly sales reports?
- His dad sat in the waiting room while he interviewed for a job?
- His dad called your supervisor to complain about you?

Stop and think about it. Are you sabotaging the development of your child's adaptive skills by doing things he should be doing for himself? Are you giving him a vote of "no confidence" when it comes to dealing with life? Are you denying him the opportunity to learn from his mistakes?

In four or five short years, your child will be entering the workforce. At that time, he will need to have the skills employers want. The most valued skills employers consistently say they are looking for include the following:

- Adaptability
- Commitment
- Communication
- Cooperation
- Being a team player
- Customer focus
- Dependability
- Honesty
- Integrity
- Initiative
- Innovation
- Quality focus
- Engagement

What is your child's portfolio when it comes to demonstrating these skills? What are you doing as a parent to help your child develop these key skills?

CHAPTER 8

Calculating College Costs

Unless you have $150,000 stashed away in a recession-proof safety deposit box, you are probably planning to borrow money to pay for your child's college education. How much you should borrow depends on who has to repay the money and how they are going to do so.

Reality Check on College Borrowing

If you, as a parent, are planning to pay off your child's student loans, you need to discuss this with a financial advisor before you sign the papers. A $30,000 loan for college at 6.8 percent interest will mean a monthly student loan payment of approximately $345 a month for 10 years. The interest on the loan will be $11,500. This will be a total cash outlay for you of approximately $41,500.

Financial advisors are quick to point out that this money—$345 per month—could be going toward your retirement account. They caution you against borrowing against your retirement. They point out that there are education loans for students but no retirement loans for parents.

But if you plan on your child paying off her student loan after college, both you and your child need to know about the 8 percent rule.

This is another guideline financial advisors use. It states that your child's student loan payments should not exceed 8 percent of her monthly gross income after graduation.

To calculate the amount to borrow, your child should multiply her estimated gross income before withholdings by .08 to determine the maximum payment she can afford. According to the 8 percent rule, a college graduate will need to earn at least $51,786 per year or $24.90 per hour to afford the $345-a-month student loan payment on a borrowed amount of $30,000.

The 8 percent rule enables your child to determine her student loan "debt threshold." This is the amount she will be able to afford to pay on student loans after college and still pay her other bills.

You need to determine your parent debt threshold as well. Financial advisors recommend that payments on your total household debt not make up more than 35 percent of your yearly household gross pay. If your family income is $100,000 a year and your total debt payments for your mortgage, car, and credit card payments are $20,000, you will be able to take on an additional $15,000 a year, or $1,250 a month, in payments for college and stay within the 35 percent rule.

Looking at debt threshold in this way raises several issues. One is that undecided students borrowing to pay for college have no idea of what their expected gross income will be after graduation. They have no realistic way to estimate how much they will be able to afford in student loans. A student loan payment of $345 a month will have a very different impact on the short-term and long-term finances of a chemical engineering major with a starting salary of $65,000 per year and an education major with a starting salary of $32,000 per year.

The 8 percent rule connects the amount your child should borrow (or will be able to repay comfortably) with the marketability of a college major. Not all majors are equal in the job market. Parents and students are rarely encouraged to think of the marketability of a major before they determine how much to borrow. College marketing promotes the fact that college graduates can expect to make almost $800,000 more than high school graduates over the total number of years in the workforce.

This is not exactly accurate. The long-term economic value of a college degree is determined by the needs of the job market and whether there is a demand for the skill set of the major in the economy. It is not determined by the level of the degree—B.A. or M.A.—itself. Student loans must be repaid with earnings generated in the short-term—the first ten years after college graduation—and not with the money earned over a lifetime.

Another problem that can arise when families look at their debt threshold is that the amount they can afford to pay in monthly payments for college may be less than the monthly parent loan payments on the amount they need to borrow for a child to attend certain schools. This becomes apparent to families as they review the child's financial aid award letters.

A financial aid award letter is a communication, either on paper or online, that details the financial aid package the college has assembled to help you fill the gap between your expected family contribution (EFC) and the cost of attendance at that school (COA).

The EFC is the amount the federal government determines a family should be able to contribute to a student's college education. It is based on information families submit on the FAFSA, the Free Application for Federal Student Aid. The EFC is used by financial aid officers to determine a student's gross financial need. The COA is the official amount that the college has determined is the cost of attending the college, including tuition, fees, and other expenses.

Since there is no standardized format for financial aid award letters and no standardized definitions of terms, many parents find it extremely difficult to compare financial aid awards and even more difficult to figure out exactly how much an institution will cost.

Here is an example of a financial aid award for Susie Smith:

Acme University Financial Aid Award	
Total Cost of Attendance:	$20,000
Expected Family Contribution:	$ 5,000
Outside Scholarship:	$ 1,000
Total Financial Need:	$14,000
Financial Assistance Offered by Acme U	
Federal Pell Grant	$ 0
State Scholarship Grant	$2,000
Institutional Grant	$7,000
Federal Work-Study	$2,000
Federal Perkins Loan	$1,500
Federal Stafford Loan—Sub.	$1,500
Total Award	$14,000
Unmet Financial Need:	$0

Acme University has assembled a package of need-based grants and loans to help Susie pay for Acme U. The EFC that Acme used to calculate Susie's financial need was based on the information Susie's parents, Stuart and Lori, submitted on the FAFSA. Using a formula based on the Smith family's income and assets, the government calculated that the Smiths should contribute $5,000 a year toward Susie's college education.

The financial aid officer at Acme U used the EFC to calculate Susie's gross financial need of $14,000. This is the difference between Acme's official COA and the Smiths' EFC based on their FAFSA and deducting the amount of the outside scholarship Susie won from her grandfather's union, Transit Workers Local #387. Acme is required to deduct any outside scholarship money a student receives from the need-based aid Acme awards.

After Acme determined Susie's gross financial need, the financial aid officer assembled a package of grants, loans, and work-study aid to cover the $14,000 in unmet need. This package included a $2,000 state scholarship grant based on Susie's high school grade point average (GPA) and class rank, a federal Perkins loan of $1,500 a year, a federal Stafford loan of $1,500, and a work-study award of $2,000 a year. To keep the state scholarship, Susie will need to maintain a 3.0 GPA. To keep the entire work-study award, she will need to work 19.5 hours a week on campus. The Smiths understand that the work-study money will be paid directly to Susie. It will not be applied to tuition, room, and board (the direct costs of college) unless Susie writes a check from her work-study money to pay for these direct costs. Otherwise, the work-study money will go directly to Susie to use for her indirect expenses. In addition, if Susie works less than the 19.5 hours a week, she will earn less money.

Now the balance Susie needs to attend Acme U is $7,000. Acme U covers this unmet need by awarding Susie a $7,000 institutional grant from its endowment. This institutional grant requires that Susie maintain a 3.25 GPA in order to renew the grant each year.

The net cost of Acme University for the Smith family is $5,000 per year. Net cost is the difference between the cost of attendance and all the financial aid Susie has been awarded. The out-of-pocket cost of Acme University for the Smith family is $8,000 per year. This is the difference between the cost of attendance and all the gift aid and work-study aid that Susie received, which totals $12,000.

To summarize, the cost for Susie Smith to attend Acme U is

1. $5000 per year in family contribution from cash, savings, or non-need-based loans. If the Smiths don't have $5,000 a year in savings or cash on hand, they will have to borrow it. Susie may be eligible for federal non-need-based loans to cover part of this amount. Stuart and Lori may be eligible for a federal Parent PLUS loan. The Smiths can also check out private loans, home equity loans, and borrowing money from relatives.
2. $3,000 per year borrowed in need-based federal Perkins and Stafford loans.
3. Working 19.5 work hours a week on campus to earn the work-study money.
4. Maintaining a 3.25 college GPA to keep the $7,000 institutional grant each year.
5. Maintaining a 3.0 college GPA to keep the $2,000 state scholarship each year.

In addition, if the cost of attendance amount used in Acme's calculations underrepresents the actual cost of attending Acme U, Susie and her family will need to come up with additional money to cover Susie's expenses.

Different colleges organize and label financial aid award information in different ways in their financial aid award letters. Some use a category called "Self-Help Aid" to include the federal work-study awards, federal Perkins loans, and federal Stafford loans under the same category. In addition, different institutions include different items in the official COA. One school might include room and board while another leaves it out.

Because of the confusion financial aid awards can generate, you need to do your own "apples to apples" comparison to find out what is really going on. You can do this by completing the Actual College Cost worksheet, using your financial aid award letter and the college's Web site. The following items address the data you need to gather to complete the Actual College Cost worksheet.

Actual College Cost	
Cost of Attendance	**Total/yr.**
1. Tuition	
2. Room and Board	
3. Books and Supplies	
4. Institutional Fees	
5. Personal Expenses	
6. Transportation	
7. Total COA (1+2+3+4+5+6)	
Gift Aid	**Amount**
8. Grants: Federal	
9. Grants: State	
10. Grants: Institutional, Other	
11. Institutional Scholarships/Awards	
12. Outside Scholarships/Awards	
13. Total Gift Aid (8+9+10+11+12)	
Self-Help Aid	**Amount**
14. Federal Work-Study	
15. Institutional Work-Study	
16. Total Self-Help Aid (14+15)	
17. Total Out of Pocket Expense: (7–13–16)	

Current Income	Amount
18. Yearly College Savings Contribution	
19. Tuition Payment Plan	
20. Yearly Parent Contribution	
21. Yearly Student Contribution	
22. Total Current Income (18+19+20+21)	
23. **Balance Needed for College:** (17–22)	

Loans	Amount
24. Federal Perkins Loan	
25. Federal Stafford Loan—Subsidized	
26. Federal Direct Loan—Subsidized	
27. Total Need-Based Loans (24+25+26)	
28. Federal Stafford Loan—Unsubsidized	
29. Federal Direct Loan—Unsubsidized	
30. Federal Parent PLUS Loan	
31. Private Loans—Parent	
32. Private Loans—Student	
33. Total Non-Need-Based Loans (28+29+30+31+32)	
34. **Total All Loans** (27+33)	
35. Balance (23–34)	

Cost of Attendance (COA)

First, do your own cost of attendance calculations. Do not use the COA listed in the financial aid award letter. Your child's actual costs may be greater or less than the official amount used by the college to calculate financial aid. Write down how much you think your child would be spending in each COA category, especially room and board, personal expenses, and miscellaneous institutional fees. You can find the institutional fees listed on the college Web site or ask the college to give you a list.

Institutional fees can include parking fees, media-technology fees, security deposits, upgraded meal plan fees, sporting event fees, student activity fees, student union fees, academic program fees, lab course fees, fitness center fees, student health insurance fees if student health insurance is mandatory, orientation fees, transcript fees, graduation fees, and so on. These can add up to $500 or more per semester. Personal expenses can include meals not on the meal plan, a personal computer, spring break trips, and sorority or fraternity fees, as well as study-abroad fees and extra travel costs. Books will be at least $500 a semester.

Gift Aid

Next, identify the "free" money listed in the financial aid award letter. Gift aid is money your child won't have to pay back. Gift aid includes federal and state grants; institutional and outside scholarships, grants, and awards; and outside scholarships, grants, and awards. You may have to decipher the acronyms used for each award. If you are not sure if an award item is a gift or a loan, ask the financial aid officer at the college for clarification. Post the gift aid amounts on the corresponding lines on the Actual College Cost worksheet. Include any tuition reimbursement money provided by an employer in this category.

Self-Help Aid

Next, put in work-study amounts. This is the maximum amount the college has allotted for work-study payments. Your child will have to work a corresponding number of hours to get the full amount. If she works less in a given semester, she will receive less. The relationship between time worked and money earned may seem obvious to you, but it is important that your child understand this as well.

In addition, remember that work-study money is paid to the student and not to the college. As money paid to the student, it helps with the indirect cost of college but does not apply to the direct costs—tuition, fees, or room and board—unless your child pays the money back to the college out of the work-study check.

Out-of-Pocket Expense

When you subtract the gift aid and self-help aid from the cost of attendance, you have your total out-of-pocket expense. This is the amount you need to come up with through savings, cash, loans, and extra scholarship money per year for your child to attend this particular institution.

Current Family Income Available for College

The next step is to assess your current financial situation as it relates to paying for college. Here you are not looking at the EFC on the award letter. You are looking at what you actually have, on hand, to pay for college. What is the amount in your current college savings or 529 college savings plan? Divide this by the number of years you expect your child to be in college. If your child requires remedial courses, add an extra semester to your calculations.

Next, determine any additional amount you can afford to pay monthly or quarterly to the college in the form of a tuition payment plan. Note this on the Actual College Cost worksheet.

Beyond a tuition payment amount, note any money you plan to contribute to your child's living expenses while in college. This is your yearly parent contribution. In this category, include a dollar amount for the money you already are spending each month to support your child while she is in high school. You are paying for food, clothing, personal expenses, insurance, cell phone, laundry, and so on. How much is this? You will continue to pay this amount to cover those same needs while your child is in college. If you think you are paying $300 a month already for your child's room/board and personal expenses, put $3000 on the worksheet ($300 × 10 months in an academic year) under yearly parent contribution. You don't want to borrow money for living expenses that you are already paying out of your current monthly budget.

Finally, put your student's contribution on the worksheet. This is an amount from summer jobs and college savings that your student will be able to contribute to her college education. Remember that if your child has a work-study award, that time commitment will limit the amount of time she has for other part-time employment during the academic year.

Once you have this much of the Actual College Cost worksheet completed, subtract the total current income amount from the total out-of-pocket expense. This is what you will need to borrow in student and parent loans for your child to attend this college.

Loans Needed to Pay for College

The loans the college has identified as available to you are listed on the financial aid award letter. Break these out into need-based loans and non-need-based loans on the Actual Cost of College worksheet.

Federal loans can be either need based or non-need based. Need-based loans are awarded to cover the difference between what college costs and what the family can reasonably afford to pay, as determined by the government's FAFSA calculations and resulting EFC. Need-based loans are subsidized, which means the federal government pays the interest on the loan while the student is in school. Non-need-based loans can be federal loans or private loans. With a federal loan that is non-need based, such as an unsubsidized Stafford loan or a parent PLUS loan, the government does not pay the interest on the loan while the student is in school. The interest accumulates. It is capitalized, which means that the interest is added to the principal and future interest is calculated on the total amount.

Any subsidized federal loans for which your child qualifies should be listed on the financial aid award letter. Here, as with grants on the award letter, the terminology can get confusing. This is because colleges sometimes refer to the student loans they are offering by the name of the loan and sometimes call them by the name of the loan program used by the college to provide the loan. A Stafford loan that is unsubsidized might be referred to as "Federal Stafford Loan Unsub" on one award letter and "Federal Direct Loan Unsub" on another. In both cases, the student is being offered a Stafford loan that is unsubsidized. (The government will not pay the interest on the loan while the student is in school.) In the first case, the loan is being offered through the FFEL (Federal Family Education Loan) program. In the second case, the loan is being offered through the William D. Ford Federal Direct Loan program.

The names of federally backed education loans are Perkins, Stafford, Plus, and Consolidation. These are offered through the Perkins, Direct, and FFEL programs. Each college chooses which federal loan programs to participate in. The main difference to the student between a Direct loan and an FFEL loan is who the student is borrowing the money from and who the student will make loan payments to after leaving school. If a Stafford loan is offered through the Direct loan program, the student is borrowing the money directly from the federal government and will make payments directly to the government after graduation. If a Stafford loan is offered through the FFEL program, the student is borrowing the money from a bank or other lending institution and will make payments to that bank or lending institution after leaving school.

Unsubsidized federal loans may or may not be listed on the award letter. This is because they are not based on need, and the purpose of the college's financial aid award is to meet need. Unsubsidized loans, however, are available to everybody. Because of this, if federal unsubsidized student loans and federal unsubsidized parent loans are not listed on the financial aid award letter, ask the financial aid office to help you identify any unsubsidized loans for which you qualify. These loans are likely to have a lower interest rate than private loans. Before you sign on for private loans, make sure you aren't eligible for federal unsubsidized loans.

At the end of the Actual Cost of College worksheet, if you have any balance left, you will need to go back and rework your numbers. Are there ways you can cut expenses? Are there additional monies you can use for college? Can you go back to the college and negotiate more aid? Do you need to regroup and consider a less expensive school?

Once you have evaluated the monetary value of your student's financial aid award letters, you should evaluate the non-tangible criteria important to you as well. The prestige of the institution and the perceived personal and professional connections that you hope your child will make as a result of attending a certain school all factor heavily into the college decision.

Other Things to Consider

Choosing a college is a highly emotional decision in many families. Many parents have deep convictions about the "door-opening" advantages of an undergraduate degree from certain schools. You need to put these expectations out on the table. What do you expect to happen differently if your child goes to college A versus college B? How will she be better off? Given that a student who is admitted to a selective or highly selective institution has strong academic and personal skills to begin with, how will attending one school make her more successful than she would be going somewhere else?

As you consider how much debt to take on to pay for college, it is helpful to ask yourself some of the questions high school counselors often use in introducing parents of high school juniors to the college admissions process:

1. Did you go to college?
2. Did you attend an Ivy League school?
3. Do you consider yourself happy and successful?
4. What is the educational background of the people in your life who are happy and successful?

Your answers to these questions will help you guide your child in choosing a college and evaluating the cost/benefit ratio of each of the colleges your child is considering.

After doing the exercises in this chapter, you probably recognize that a big way to save money on college is for your child to make the most of high school. How can you help your child make the right choices in high school to ensure college success?

Parent Tip 45

The actual cost of attendance for your child may be greater or less than the official cost of attendance used by the college to calculate financial need. This is why you and your child should do your own cost of college calculation before accepting any financial aid award.

A student attending college and living at home would need to borrow less money to pay for college than a student living on campus. The COA upon which student loans are based often includes the cost of room and board. The loan amount is more than the student needs to cover the cost of living at home. In addition, your child's personal expenses can be greater or less than the personal expenses included in the COA.

Personal expenses can include, among other things, entertainment, spring break trips, campus sporting-event fees, sorority and fraternity fees, and food not included in the meal plan. Add these up to determine the true cost of attendance for your child.

Your child can accept or reject any or all of the loans offered in a financial aid award letter. If your child does not need to borrow the full amount of loans offered, she needs to communicate back to the college that she is not accepting the full amount.

Parent Tip 46

Many parents and young adults see debt for college as "good debt." Along with a home mortgage and a small-business loan, a student loan is seen as creating value. The value of a student loan is the anticipated increased earning power for the student who has a college degree.

"Good debt" is contrasted with "bad debt." Any credit purchase that does not increase in value is bad debt. Using credit cards to pay for meals out and spring break trips is considered bad debt. The value of the purchase has depreciated or evaporated before the first payment is due.

The problem is that more and more students are graduating from college today with significant amounts of both good debt and bad debt. They are entering the job market burdened with both student loan and credit card debt. This can limit or delay their ability to take on additional good debt for a home mortgage later on.

In thinking about the good debt value of student loans, you need to help your child analyze the impact of student loan debt in two ways: the manageability of the monthly loan payment in the immediate years after graduation and the interest paid on the loan over time.

A $30,000 loan for college will mean your child will be paying $345 a month over ten years. The total interest your child will pay over ten years will be approximately $11,500. If your child chooses a 25-year repayment plan, the monthly payment will be $208 a month over 25 years, and the interest paid will be $32,500.

This loan payment may seem manageable to you and your child. The interest rate on the student loan, compared to credit card rates, may make a student

(continued)

(continued)

loan seem like inexpensive money. But interest paid on good debt in the form of student loans is money that will not be available to spend on other good debt later on. In addition, many of the consumer protections you associate with other forms of debt, such as auto loans, credit card balances, and home mortgages, are limited with student loans.

Be very cautious in encouraging your child to take on more student loan debt than she will be able to handle. You do not want your child to start adult life with so much "good debt" in the form of student loans that she is unable to take on other "good debt" in the form of a home mortgage when the time comes. You don't want your child to have credit problems later on due to difficulty paying student loans.

Parent Tip 47

Most financial aid offers today are prepackaged. This means they are presented to students and parents as a total aid amount, which the student then accepts or modifies. This is called "passive acceptance."

Because financial aid awards often include both grants and loans, it is easy for student and parents to confuse the "aid" in a financial aid award and the portion that is actually lightly subsidized consumer debt.

One way to think of this is to define aid as money you don't have to pay back. This would include grants, including the Pell grant, state grants, and scholarships. Debt is money you do have to pay back. This would include federally backed student loans and private loans.

Over the past 20 years, there has been a shift in the composition of many student-aid awards. Colleges have offered less in gift aid and more in student loan aid.

Subsidized student loans are debt on which the interest is deferred until your child leaves college and has to begin paying back the loan. The "aid" part of a subsidized loan is the deferred interest on the loan, the lower interest rate, and the ease of borrowing for someone who has a limited credit history.

Unsubsidized student loans are debt on which the interest accrues each month while your child is in college. The "aid" part of an unsubsidized loan is a lower interest rate and the ease of borrowing in comparison to borrowing from a private lender.

Student loans have to be repaid whether or not your child finishes college and whether or not she is able to find a college-level job upon graduation. "How much financial aid can I get?" on the front end of the college-admissions process is a very different question from "How much financial aid do I have to repay?" on the back end of your child's college experience.

Make sure both you and your child understand exactly how much your child is borrowing and how the money will be spent. Sit down with your child before she chooses a college and make sure that both of you understand the full implication of each financial aid award your child is offered.

Parent Tip 48

Most colleges and universities have sophisticated enrollment management plans that include strategies and tactics to help the institution shape enrollment (size, diversity, SAT/ACT scores, desired majors) and meet its financial goals. Enrollment management uses technology to analyze data; predict trends; evaluate the potential success of applicants; and systematically communicate with prospective students, parents, alumni, and donors. It often combines college marketing, recruiting, registration, retention, and financial aid under one administrative umbrella.

Scholarships and grants are often used as tools in enrollment management. This means they are awarded to prospective students strategically to help the college meet its enrollment management goals.

Merit-based aid is financial aid awarded for a student's accomplishments, whether academic, artistic, or athletic; for the student's non-curricular activities and achievements; or for any criteria set up by the person, family, or organization that funds the award. Merit-based aid can be an athletic scholarship, a music or drama scholarship, a community service award, or a unique scholarship open only to students who meet certain criteria such as "all red-haired women of German descent interested in mechanical engineering."

Institutional scholarships are merit-based aid offered by the college. *Outside scholarships are* merit-based aid awarded by donors outside the college or the government, including service organizations, employers, and foundations. Merit-based aid is awarded to selected students, regardless of their financial need or assets.

Institutional grants differ from scholarships in that they are often need based rather than merit based. Institutional grants are financial aid awards to help a student make up the difference between what the student has been awarded in other financial aid, including state and federal grants, federal loans, and scholarships, and what the student still needs to pay in order to attend the college. The money to fund institutional grants usually comes from the college's budget, endowment, or income. In some cases, the grant is simply a tuition discount that reduces the sticker price of the college for selected students.

(continued)

(continued)

Both grants and scholarships are free money in the sense that they do not have to be repaid by the student. They usually have strings attached, however, in that the student must meet certain GPA and other requirements to get the money each semester. Because the terminology around grants and scholarships can be so confusing, make sure that both you and your child clearly understand the terms of any scholarship or grant your child accepts.

Parent Tip 49

Most young adults overestimate the salary they will be making when they graduate from college and underestimate the extra expenses they will incur while in college. This combination of miscalculations results in students using credit cards to pay for unanticipated college expenses. The credit card debt must then be paid off with a post-college salary that is less than the student expected.

Encourage your child to research the salary she can realistically expect starting out in a particular career. Have her research the median salary for her career, and recognize that starting out she will probably be making less than the median. In 2008, the median salary of all full-time U.S. workers was $32,390 per year, or $15.57 per hour. Half of all workers made above that amount and half made below, including workers with years of experience.

Your child needs to be honest, before going to college, about anticipated extra expenses—books, entertainment, transportation, spring break trips, and campus organization and event fees. Only with this information will your child be able to limit credit card debt and control her overall long-term debt for college.

Parent Tip 50

Your child can live like a student while a student or live like a student after graduation.

Your child's student loan payment will have a direct impact on the quality of her lifestyle after college. A student loan payment of $345 a month can mean the difference between having an apartment or living at home with Mom and Dad.

Both you and your child need to keep the end in mind. It is not financially responsible to live on student loans. Encourage your child to borrow for educational needs, not lifestyle wants. You do not want your child to start her work life trapped by student loan debt that is difficult to repay.

Parent Tip 51

One reason for the rise of helicopter parenting today is the mixed message colleges send to parents about parental involvement.

On the one hand, parents are expected to be very involved in paying for college. There is no way that a student who is claimed as a dependent on his parents' tax returns can go through the financial aid process alone. Parents have to turn in forms, provide signatures, and agree to parent loan repayment terms. They have to work closely with college personnel to process financial aid, and this interaction has to take place every year. Financial aid is not a "drop him off at college and let him go" experience.

On the other hand, parents are expected to be hands-off when it comes to the dynamics of the classroom. A student who hands his cell phone to his instructor and says, "My dad wants to talk to you about my grade" is not likely to get a positive response. Parental intervention is considered interference by professors and a sign that the parent is not willing to let the student become an adult.

You need to clarify the boundaries in your own mind. Stay out of the classroom, whether the location is on campus or online. Go into the administration building only after your child has attempted to solve the problem himself.

Parent Tip 52

If your child is planning on taking out student loans to attend a particular college or university, have her talk to someone who graduated from the same college four years earlier. Use your network of family, friends, co-workers, and high school counselors to identify students who attended schools of interest.

A recent graduate of an institution will have a different perspective on the cost/benefit ratio of student loans to young adult lifestyle. Have your child find out what that young person would have done differently when it comes to borrowing and spending student loans.

Parent Tip 53

Many parents find it more difficult to talk to a child about family finances than to talk to him or her about sex. But it is important to be honest with your child, up front, about what you can and cannot afford when it comes to paying for college.

(continued)

(continued)

College recruiters will be talking to your child about college fit. This means the size of campus, the social life, the variety of extracurricular activities and organizations, the amenities on campus, and the attractions of the community in which the college is located.

Explain to your child that while fit is important to you, so is cost. Any number of colleges can be a good fit and allow your child to flourish and grow. Your job is to make sure that the college your child chooses will not cost more than either you or your child can afford.

A big part of what you are teaching your child through the college-search process is financial literacy. Your job is to make sure that your child doesn't get in over her head with college costs.

In taking on student loans for an undergraduate degree, your child will be assuming a level of consumer debt that you probably did not have when you left college. You may have to clarify that your family's financial situation is different from how your child perceives it. Be honest with your child about your own finances in order to do the right thing by all concerned in the college-selection process.

Parent Tip 54

In considering how much money to borrow with student loans, the two questions you and your child must answer are "How much am I borrowing?" and "Why am I borrowing this amount?"

This gets into budgeting. Both you and your child will need a budget to determine how much you each can borrow and how much you each can repay.

If you aren't experienced at making a budget, there are many resources online to help you and your child get started. To find some good examples, do an Internet search for the words "budget worksheets for college students."

In addition, if your child will be getting a refund check from a student loan disbursement, she needs to know how that refund check will be spent. What expenses beyond tuition and books will the refund cover? Make sure your child is using student loans to pay for college needs and not for lifestyle wants.

Parent Tip 55

You don't have to accept all the loans offered in the financial aid award letter. You can accept or reject all or part of the loan amounts you are offered.

If you have a college savings plan that will cover $2,000 a year of your child's college expenses and the unmet financial need amount on the financial aid award letter is $0, you can reduce the amount of loans your child takes out by $2,000. The key is to communicate back to the college that you do not want the full loan amount the college has offered.

Parent Tip 56

One thing that has changed since you were in school is the attractiveness of student loans to lenders.

When Congress established the Guaranteed Student Loan Program in 1965, the intent was to help financially needy students go to college. Because these students often had no credit history or collateral, they were considered high-risk borrowers by lenders. Banks and other financial institutions were reluctant to lend them money. From a loan manager's perspective, the bank couldn't repossess an education or foreclose on a college degree, so it was risky business to lend students money.

Because of this reluctance to lend, Congress passed additional legislation to make it more attractive to lenders to lend students the money for college, setting up loan guarantee organizations to buy up student loans from banks so that the banks could lend more money. The government also agreed to reimburse lenders if the student defaulted on their loans and ensure that lenders would get good interest rates regardless of the going market rates.

With the dramatic rise in the cost of a college education over the last 25 years, student loans became more in demand and a lucrative business for lenders. The student loan industry expanded, and some of the larger loan companies began to buy up other companies related to student loans, such as loan-processing companies, collection agencies, student loan consolidation companies, college savings plan companies, and higher education consulting firms advising colleges on how to use financial aid as a recruitment tool.

In recent years, Congress has passed legislation that reduced subsidies to lenders, which resulted in many lenders exiting the student loan industry. More legislation is currently under review that would further change the relationship between borrowers, lenders, and the federal government.

Because of all this, you need to be a prudent consumer of higher education. Higher education at all levels—trade schools, proprietary schools, community colleges, four-year colleges and universities, and graduate school programs—is a large and sophisticated financial business. As a parent, you need to understand

(continued)

(continued)

how you are spending your money, what you hope to get out of your investment, and the terms of every financial document you sign before you sign it. You need to put your short-term decisions about borrowing money for college into your long-term vision of what you want for your child when he leaves college, both in terms of the opportunities you hope he will have as well as the limits he will experience due to student loan debt. The College Loan Worksheet will help you track your current loans in more detail.

College Loan Worksheet

Total	Amount	Payment	Interest Rate	Years
Federal Perkins Loan				
Federal Stafford Loan—Subsidized				
Federal Direct Loan—Subsidized				
Federal Stafford Loan—Unsubsidized				
Federal Direct Loan—Unsubsidized				
Federal PLUS Loan				
Private Loan—Parent				
Private Loan—Student				
Federal Consolidation Loan				
Private Consolidation Loan				
Total Debt: All Loans				

College Loan Worksheet—Summary
Total Loan Debt: $
Monthly Loan Payment: $
Expected Gross Monthly Salary: $
.08 × Gross Monthly Salary: $

Parent Tip 57

Surveys indicate that two-thirds of parents say their college-age children have no understanding of how much college will cost. When these young people take on student loans to pay for college, financial ignorance can become financial hardship when students leave school with loan debt they have no way to repay.

Your parental tax returns will be required for the college to determine your dependent child's student loan eligibility. Therefore, the best time to discuss college costs with your child is when you use your income tax records to complete the FAFSA form each year. Tax time is when you need to have a conversation with your child about the total amount your child has borrowed, what the monthly payment will be on those existing loans, and how much additional money your child can comfortably borrow. You can use the College Loan Worksheet to guide this conversation.

Parent Tip 58

One of the most misleading pieces of advice is that a student should not borrow more in student loans than the amount of his expected yearly gross income after college. This would suggest that an education major anticipating a first-year teaching job paying $30,000 per year could comfortably borrow $30,000 in student loans. In fact, this is only true if he takes 25 years to repay the loan.

The monthly payment on a student loan debt of $30,000, assuming a 6.8 percent interest rate over 10 years, would be $345 per month. This payment would eat up 13.8 percent of the student's monthly gross income. The actual amount the student owes—loan plus interest—is $41,428. This is the amount upon which the monthly loan payment is calculated, not the $30,000 borrowed. A student would need to make $51,786 per year to stay within the 8 percent rule and pay off the $30,000 loan in 10 years. If the student extended the payments over 25 years,

(continued)

(continued)

the monthly payment would be reduced to $208, with a total of $32,466 interest added to the $30,000 student loan. Over 25 years, a student loan of $30,000 will cost the student $62,466.

The 8 percent rule is a much safer way to calculate how much to borrow. A student making $30,000 after graduation can afford a $201 per month student loan payment, which means she should limit her borrowing to $17,500 to pay for college.

Parent Tip 59

There are a variety of things to consider when evaluating the impact of grants and scholarships on the cost of college. Here are some questions to ask the college or the outside scholarship provider when it comes to merit-based aid:

- Will the grant or scholarship amount be similar in subsequent years?

  Verify that the grant or scholarship will be renewed for the same amount each year, provided your family financial situation is the same.

- What is the college's outside scholarship policy?

  You must report any outside scholarships to the colleges you are considering, as the scholarships may reduce the amount of federal and institutional need-based aid you are awarded, including student loans.

- What is the GPA necessary to keep this scholarship or award?

  Make sure both you and your child understand the terms of each scholarship or award, including the number of credit hours your child will need to enroll in to keep the scholarship as well as the GPA that must be maintained and the number of hours the student must work.

- Can the scholarship be regained if I lose it?

  You need to understand what happens if your child loses the scholarship. Many parents are stunned when a strong high school student fails to meet the criteria for scholarship renewal. High school success is not the same as college readiness. The first year of college is a major transition for students. They must work without the direction, discipline, and support they experienced from high school teachers. It takes some young people time to get their academic bearings. You need to have a contingency plan to pay for college if the scholarship is no longer available. Know what your options are for getting the scholarship back.

- Can my scholarships be "stacked"?

You need to find out if the scholarships your child is awarded can be used together or if accepting one scholarship means your child can't use the other scholarship at the same school. Some scholarships come with a "may not be used with other offers" qualification.

- What happens if I don't make the team or get injured while using an athletic scholarship to pay for this school?

  You need to know what happens if your child loses an athletic scholarship. Have a backup plan to pay the difference in college costs if your child decides to quit the team after several years to focus more on school and work.

- Will the scholarship amount increase as the cost of college increases?

  This is unlikely, but it's good to ask.

Parent Tip 60

One problem parents encounter in trying to get a handle on college costs is that many colleges will not consider a student for any type of financial assistance until the student has applied for admission to the school. Since applying to many schools is both expensive and time consuming, you probably want to narrow the list. The FAFSA4caster can help you do this.

The FAFSA4caster is a free online tool developed by the U.S. Department of Education. It provides students with an early estimate of their eligibility for federal student aid. Using the FAFSA4caster, the college's Web site, your child's high school transcript, the state's department of higher education Web site, and a list of any outside scholarships you think your child could earn, you can get a basic idea of where your child would stand in relation to paying for a college by filling out the Actual College Cost worksheet.

First, complete the FAFSA4caster, which you can find by doing an online search for FAFSA4caster. The FAFSA4caster will give you an estimate of any federal grants, loans, and work-study amounts your child will be eligible to receive. It will also tell you your official government expected family contribution (EFC), which all colleges will be using in determining your financial need.

Next, get an unofficial copy of your child's high school transcript from the high school. This is what your child brings to the table when it comes to earning scholarships and grants. It shows you your child's official GPA and class rank and any ACT or SAT scores your child has already achieved. Using this information, you can research the state grants and scholarships your child is eligible for based on

(continued)

(continued)

class rank, GPA, and test scores. These state grants and scholarships will be listed on your state's department of higher education Web site.

The next step is to use your child's high school transcript and the college financial aid Web site to determine if there are any automatic academic scholarships and grants offered by the college for which your child will qualify. These automatic scholarships and grants may be based on GPA, class rank, test scores, or other criteria, such as community service hours. In addition, the college's financial aid Web site will help you identify any competitive scholarships your child could apply for at that school.

Finally, locate the cost of attendance information on the college's Web site. Put all the information you have gathered on the appropriate lines on the Actual College Cost worksheet. If you know the amount of an outside scholarship your child might qualify for, put that down as well. Keep in mind that the amount of the outside scholarship may be deducted from the amount the college allots as need-based aid. In other words, an outside scholarship could lower the amount your child is eligible to borrow in federal need-based loans or the amount of grants she is awarded by the college in institutional aid.

With all this information, you will have a better idea of how much additional money in institutional grants and scholarships, college savings, cash, and additional outside scholarships you will need for your child to attend this college. Ask recruiters the median amount of scholarship or institutional grant money the college awards each year. Here you want to know the median amount of free money the college awards, not the median amount of financial aid the college awards, since financial aid often includes both loans and grants. Factor this figure into your calculations. Identify how much in student and parent loans you would potentially need to borrow for your child to attend this school. Completing this exercise using the FAFSA4caster can help you decide which colleges fit your financial profile.

Parent Tip 61

The interest on unsubsidized federal loans is capitalized, meaning that any unpaid interest is added to the principal balance and interest is charged on the new amount. This increases total debt and can have a significant impact on the amount of student loan payment a young adult faces after graduation.

If a student borrows a total of $18,000 over four years of college, the monthly payment would be $207 a month over 10 years if the student paid the interest while in college. If the student did not pay the interest while in college, the monthly payment would be $244 a month. The total interest paid on an $18,000 unsubsidized loan for college, if the student paid the interest during college, would be $9857. The total interest would be $11,284 if the student did not pay the interest while in school.

Parent Tip 62

Like the back of credit card statements, student loan documents are detailed, dull, and difficult to read, but it is very important that you and your child understand the terms of the loan documents you are signing. In particular, make sure you know the answers to these consumer protection questions before you or your child sign any loan document:

- Can I pre-pay this loan without penalty?
- What is the interest rate? Is it fixed or variable?
- If it is a variable rate, is there a ceiling on the interest rate?
- If my child misses payments on this loan, will it impact my credit rating?
- What happens if I am late with a payment? Are there any late fees charged? Does my interest rate go up? If so, is there a way for me to regain the lower interest rate?
- What happens if I lose my job? Can I make arrangements to stop payments? If so, will I be charged interest?
- What are all the circumstances in this loan agreement under which the company can change my rate?
- If I default on this loan, can the company claim my other assets, including car and wages? Can I discharge this loan in bankruptcy?

Parent Tip 63

Make sure you know the financial aid deadlines and paperwork required for the colleges you are seriously considering.

Most financial aid is awarded on a first-come, first-served basis. To ensure maximum consideration for federal, state, and institutional aid, check information from each school to determine the required application materials and financial aid application deadlines. Complete your FAFSA as soon as you have your taxes done each year.

(continued)

(continued)

In addition, if your family economic circumstances change or if the amount of aid offered seems out of line with your financial situation, contact the financial aid administrator at the college. Financial aid officers often have leeway to adjust awards based on their professional judgment.

Parent Tip 64

The rates on student loans vary. The federal government is scheduled to lower the interest rate on need-based student loans in the next few years.

It is important to understand that if interest rates go down but the cost of college continues to go up, your student loan debt may ultimately be the same.

You need to look at the big picture of the cost of college over four or more years. How much has the official cost of college at this institution increased each year over the last four years? What is the average number of years it takes a student to graduate from this institution? Consider this information, along with interest rate on student loans, when deciding how much money to borrow with student loans.

Parent Tip 65

The federal EFC is not the same thing as the profile EFC used by some colleges to calculate financial need. The federal EFC is a calculated estimate of how much a student and his parents can contribute toward college costs. Individual colleges and universities, as well as private scholarship providers, may do need calculations in a different way.

Ask the college which EFC it will be using in calculating your student's financial need.

In meeting "need," whether based on a federal or profile EFC, the college will be providing a package that includes grants, loans, and work study. Even if a school provides for 100 percent of need, a substantial amount of that financial aid package could be loans.

Parent Tip 66

Like everything else in higher education, the cost of college textbooks has risen faster than the rate of inflation over the past 20 years. Parents and students increasingly are looking for alternatives to paying full price at the campus bookstore for a textbook that can sometimes cost more than $300.

Some things to look into to reduce your costs include renting books at the beginning of the semester through the campus bookstore, selling textbooks back during "buyback" days at the end of the semester, finding new and used textbooks through online booksellers, downloading e-copies of textbooks to a personal computer or handheld reading device, reading a textbook that is not downloadable by accessing it through a Web site, using textbooks loaned from the campus library, and borrowing a copy from a professor who received extra review copies from the publisher.

Some of the things that can go wrong buying textbooks from sources other than the campus bookstore include buying the wrong version of the text, not being able to get your money back if the class is canceled, and not having the book arrive in time for the first day of class. The textbooks used in a class can vary from instructor to instructor, even though the class title and number is the same. If the college changes instructors at the last minute, the textbooks used in the class section can change.

Talk to other parents about what worked for them. Make sure you understand the return policy wherever you buy the book. Consider shipping costs when comparing the price of books. Make sure your child knows the book buyback dates on campus and gets to the bookstore early on those days to get money back for textbooks.

Parent Tip 67

There are a number of excellent free college scholarship databases on the Internet. These databases have over 1.5 million scholarships worth more than $3.4 billion. Many of these scholarships are for academic merit, but there are also many scholarships for average students that recognize activities and attributes such as community service and leadership.

You do not have to pay money to find scholarships for college. Use one of the large, free searchable databases to input your student's qualifications and characteristics and see which scholarships are possibilities. Make sure you know all the application deadlines and processes. While you may not be able to make up the difference between the cost of college and your college savings with outside scholarship dollars, you will hopefully find some additional money to help defray college costs.

CHAPTER 9

Navigating Through High School

The most effective way you can contain the cost of college is to make sure your child takes a rigorous program of study in high school. This is not always as easy as it seems.

High School Diplomas and College Readiness

Many high schools today offer a smorgasbord of high school diplomas from which students and parents must choose. These options include college-prep diplomas, honors diplomas, International Baccalaureate diplomas, and basic high school diplomas. Because of the variety of choices, you as a parent can easily assume that all college-prep–sounding diplomas will ensure that your child meets the minimum high school course requirements to be accepted into most state and private institutions. You can also assume, often incorrectly, that if your child graduates from high school, he or she is ready for college.

Many high school diplomas do not require enough units of math, science, or foreign language to prepare students to begin college at the college level. When tested for course placement at the college of their choice, many students score into remedial courses in math, writing, or reading because they did not develop those skills well enough in high school to be successful in college-level work.

Remedial courses for college freshmen are among the fastest-growing segments of higher education. Called "developmental courses" or "college-prep" courses, these classes do not count towards the credit hours your child needs to complete a college degree. They are required, however, to build your child's skills up to where she can succeed in college-level courses.

One in four college freshmen now require at least one remedial course in college. Many of these students must take remedial math. This is directly related to the amount of math young people are taking in high school. Allowing your child to "opt out" of high school math is one of the most expensive mistakes that you, as a parent, can make.

Your child will need to complete at least a course in college algebra to earn a four-year college degree in any discipline today. For many majors, including business, your child will need more math than that.

College advisors, however, routinely work with students whose last math course was completed in their sophomore or junior year in high school. These students say they intend to get a four-year college degree. They are surprised and irritated to find out they have to learn the math in college they chose not to learn in high school.

There is no way your child will be ready to succeed in college algebra with two or three years of high school math, especially if that math is consumer math or algebra prep. Students with only two years of high school math will be required to take at least one, if not two, remedial math courses in order to build up to a course that will count as an elective towards a four-year degree. College algebra comes after that.

Here are some of the ways opting out of high school math can directly impact your pocketbook:

- There is the cost for the remedial courses themselves. At $80 to $800 a credit hour, plus the cost of books, remedial courses aren't cheap.
- There is the possibility of student loan eligibility problems later on. Your child can run out of loan eligibility senior year in college because she used up loan eligibility taking remedial courses freshman year.
- There is the cost of repeating remedial math classes your child can't pass because of the fast pace of instruction at the college level. Withdrawal and failure rates for remedial math classes are high because students must learn in a 16-week semester what they could have learned over a full academic year in high school.

- Lack of math prerequisites can block your child from taking other classes that require math as a prerequisite. This can throw your child behind on completing courses in a major, such as business, that has math requirements for other courses. Delays in course sequencing can easily add one or more semesters to your total college costs while your child plays catch-up with courses needed for a major.

Earning College Credit in High School

Another way to control the cost of college is to make judicious use of earning college credit in high school. Contrary to popular opinion, your child should not necessarily earn as much college credit as possible in high school. Even though college credit earned in high school costs less than the same credit earned in college, it may or may not be in your child's best interest to take the high school course for college credit.

High school students can earn college credit in several ways:

- They can enroll in an honors course in high school and take a national Advanced Placement (AP) test at the end of the course.
- They can take an honors course in high school and take an International Baccalaureate (IB) exam at the end of the course.
- They can take an honors course in high school for which they receive college credit from a local college or university. This is "dual credit."
- They can take a college course on a nearby college campus along with regularly enrolled college students.
- They can earn articulated college credit for career and technical courses taken while in high school.
- They can go to an authorized test center and take a CLEP (College Level Examination Program) test to earn college credit for certain courses, regardless of whether they have enrolled in the corresponding class in high school.

For AP credit, at the end of the honors course your child takes, and pays for, a nationally recognized test. The results are sent to the college your child decides to attend. That college determines the passing score for the AP course and decides how passing scores will be credited. Colleges may use AP courses to place students into a higher-level course or to award credits that meet degree requirements. Each college decides how many AP credits it will apply to a degree at that institution.

IB credit works like AP credit in that your child takes a standardized exam at the end of the IB course and submits the scores to a college or university. The receiving institution determines how IB credit will apply to its degrees.

With dual credit, your child signs up to take an honors course in high school for college credit. You pay the local credentialing college for the credit to be recorded on a transcript for your student. The transcript can be sent to other colleges or universities, where the course may or may not apply to your child's degree. The more selective the four-year receiving institution, the more selective it will be about accepting dual credit earned through other colleges.

If your child takes classes at a local college, she will have a college transcript from that institution that can be sent to other colleges she plans to attend. The college classes can also be transferred back to the high school to meet requirements for high school graduation. This is another form of dual credit popular with homeschooled students and their families.

Articulated credit is college credit that a student enrolled in technical classes in high school can apply to a degree or certificate at a local community college or technical school. After a student is enrolled in a community college or technical school career program, the college will give the student credit for work done in high school. For example, a student who studied computer networking in high school could earn college credit for six hours of computer science courses that are part of a computer networking certificate at a local community college.

Finally, there is CLEP credit. This is similar to AP credit in that the student takes a nationally recognized exam in a college subject. It is an option for students who have mastered the content of the course and would like to get college credit for demonstrating that knowledge on a standardized test. Each college has its own policy about the CLEP grade needed to earn credit and how many CLEP credits it will accept.

Understanding How College Credits Apply to Degrees

With any kind of college credit earned in high school, you need to consider the big picture of how the credit will apply to a college degree. There is a difference between a course counting as college credit and a course applying toward the requirements of your child's degree. All college credit earned in high school counts as college credit and is reflected on your child's transcript as a college-level course, but not all courses apply to every degree or major.

To understand this, you need to look at how a four-year college degree is structured.

A four-year degree is made up of building blocks of courses. At the foundation is a block of approximately 40 credit hours of general education courses students call "the basics." This block of courses includes college-level writing, math, communications, history, science, humanities, and social-science courses, as well as other courses considered by the college as critical to giving your child a foundation for further study and for life. They form the general education or "liberal arts core" of a degree granted by a particular college or university. They are traditionally taken during the freshman and sophomore year of college.

Next are pre-major requirements. These are courses a student is expected to take during the sophomore year in college in order to be on track for enrolling in upper-division major courses in a particular college. Business majors need to take economics and accounting courses sophomore year to be on track for other business classes junior year. English majors may need to take American literature and a foreign language sophomore year to be on track for an English major junior year. Every major has at least some courses that must be taken sophomore year to be "on track" to enter the major junior year.

After pre-major requirements come major courses. These are upper-division courses that can only be taken at a four-year school. Major courses give your child a depth of knowledge, experience, and skill in a major field of study.

Finally, there is a smaller block of "minor" or emphasis-area courses, and perhaps some general electives, that fill out the total credit hours for a four-year degree. The number of general electives required for a degree varies by major.

Credits earned in high school can apply to a college degree in one of three ways:

- As a general-education requirement
- As a pre-major requirement
- As elective credit

To determine if your child should take a course for college credit, think about why you want your child to take this particular course for credit.

- Is it to ensure your child's academic preparedness for college?
- Is it to get general education credits out of the way for less money?
- Is it to meet a pre-major requirement for a particular major?
- Is it just in case your child needs electives to fill out her degree?

Honors courses are always beneficial. The research consistently shows that the more rigorous the classes your child takes in high school, particularly in math and science, the more likely your child will be to complete a college degree. In some instances, though, a young person might be better off taking an honors course without college credit during his or her senior year in high school and completing a similar course for credit on campus freshman year.

An example would be a pharmacy major taking College Chemistry I for honors credit in high school. She will be attending college on a scholarship requiring a 3.5 GPA for renewal. If she has credit for College Chemistry I from high school, she will be enrolled in College Chemistry II as a freshman, along with other pre-pharmacy students who took College Chemistry I in college the previous year. This student might be better off repeating College Chemistry I as a freshman in college, getting a good grade because of her strong preparation in high school, and letting herself get established academically and socially before taking College Chemistry II. Doing so would protect her scholarship GPA during the transition to college.

AP credit is awarded for meeting rigorous standards set on a national exam. A student earning AP credit can be assured she has the basic content of a college-level course in the subject. With dual-credit classes, there are no national standards. The grade in the course, like the grade in any on-campus college course, is determined by how well the student meets the standards of the instructor. The college granting the dual credit oversees the curriculum and makes sure the high school teacher is qualified to teach the course at the college level.

If your child is taking a dual-credit class in high school, are you confident that the grading standards in your high school are the same as those your child would experience in college? Are you sure she will have the skills needed to succeed at the next level? Will the experience of taking U.S. History I in a high school classroom be the same as taking it on-campus freshman year? Is this a factor for you?

These are things you need to consider before spending money in high school for college credit. By completing most of the "basics" while still in high school, your child will be enrolling in sophomore-level courses freshman year. This means your child will start college competing against second-year "native" students who have already weathered the transition to college your child is now experiencing. For some students, this adds stress to an already stressful time. A student who has succeeded in an AP course or rigorous dual-credit course in high school has mastered college-level course content in a high school context. A student who has completed the same course and earned the same grade on a college campus has mastered college-level course content in a college context. For some students, adjusting to the new context of college learning while taking sophomore-level courses during freshman year is a challenge. It can impact a student's ability to maintain the GPA necessary to keep a scholarship. In addition, having freshman year out of the way puts a student that much closer to declaring a major.

Finally, if you are paying for college classes in high school just in case your child needs electives later on, you need to understand that many degrees have very specific elective requirements and need few, if any, general electives. In addition, some technical or career courses completed in high school for college credit may meet requirements for specific degree programs at specific schools, but they may not count as electives at every college or university.

In general, taking college composition and college algebra in high school is a good way to save time and money on college. Beyond taking these courses, it depends on the individual student and her academic goals. Higher education in the United States is decentralized. Each college makes its own rules about which courses apply to which degree, and often colleges within the same university make their own rules as well. Of the 16 hours of college German your child takes in high school, three might apply to an engineering degree while all 16 might apply to a journalism degree. Saying, "I want to make sure all my child's courses in high school transfer, but I don't know where she is going to college or what she wants to study" is like saying, "I want the cheapest, most direct flight to my vacation destination, but I don't know where I want to go." You probably will waste some time and money in the process.

For these reasons, you should work closely with your high school counselor in making the decision to pay for college credit earned in high school. You should also seek out additional information. Many colleges have links on their Web sites indicating which courses they will take from other colleges and how those courses will apply at their school. They also have information about their AP, IB, and CLEP test policies. A college admissions rep can help you understand this information.

Another great resource is other parents. Talk to parents who have students currently enrolled in a college your child is considering. Ask them how courses taken in high school worked out at the college level for their child. What advice can they give you based on their experience?

With more information, you will be in a much better position to decide whether taking a high school course for college credit is a good decision for your child.

But what if your child isn't taking college credit in high school? What if your child isn't interested in college at all? What do you do then?

Parent Tip 68

Many boomer-era parents have a bad attitude about math. One reason for this is that many boomers didn't have to take math as part of their college degree. As a result, adults who would never think of saying they were "never any good at reading" will casually tell everyone they are no good at math.

Think about it. Do you routinely tell people they don't need to know how to write? Do you think your parental counterparts in other countries are telling their children "Don't bother with algebra—that's what computers are for"?

Times have changed. Whether you liked math in school or not, whether you use math on your current job or not, you need to encourage your child to succeed in math. Math, science, and technology will be woven into all of the high-paying jobs of the future. You need to communicate to your child that doing well in math is important. Convey confidence in your child's ability to succeed in math even if you did not succeed in it yourself. You need to insist on high-quality math instruction in every elementary, middle, and high school that your child attends.

Parent Tip 69

Parents often face an uphill battle trying to get a high school junior or senior to continue taking math courses beyond the minimum required for high school graduation. In addition, many parents secretly question why students need algebra at all. If your child is not going to be a scientist or engineer, why does she need to learn algebra in the first place?

The answer is that all good jobs of the future, whether in business, education, or health care, will require the problem-solving skills that algebra develops. The reason your child needs to study algebra is not to memorize equations she will never use. It is to learn a disciplined process for problem-solving. Algebra teaches students to identify what they already know about a problem and then work systematically to find a solution to what they don't know. The study of algebra requires patience, persistence, and organization. It teaches students respect for the power of numbers and shows them how numbers can work for or against them as consumers, whether they are taking out a home mortgage, investing in the stock market, or paying off student loans.

Parent Tip 70

One of the main challenges you will face when you send a child off to college is to shift from being your child's advocate to being your child's teacher of self-advocacy skills. Many parents find this transition difficult. This is because they have spent years "partnering" with teachers and taking a "team approach" with school personnel.

While it may have been appropriate in elementary school for you to contact your child's teacher about a problem in a class, it is not appropriate at the college level. Your child is expected to advocate for himself.

Self-advocacy is a skill that must be taught and practiced like any other skill. Your job is to teach your child to advocate for himself. At the college level, your primary connection should be with your child, not with the professor or campus personnel. You can make suggestions to your child as to how to handle situations, what questions to ask, and ways to communicate with college personnel, but you should not be intervening in your child's day-to-day problems yourself.

Parent Tip 71

There are two simple things you can do to greatly reduce your family communication problems with a college. One is to include your child's name and student ID number in any voice mail messages you leave and in the subject line of any e-mails you or your child send. The other is to clearly articulate a return phone number twice on any voice mail left with college personnel.

Having the student ID number at hand will allow the person receiving the call to look up your child's relevant information before returning the call. A clearly articulated return phone number will eliminate delays caused by garbled messages.

Parent Tip 72

Young people today will need both education and work experience to find a good job after they leave school. Many parents increasingly expect colleges to provide access to such work experience in the form of internships.

While internships related to an academic interest are important, don't underestimate the value of your child having traditional non-internship jobs such as retail sales or restaurant service. Traditional high school and college jobs held during the academic year and in the summer teach and reinforce critical adaptive skills. Young people employed in such jobs get paid for dependability, getting along with co-workers, and accepting direction and supervision from a boss. They learn how to deal with the boring but necessary "administrivia" that is part of every job—the routine paperwork that must be completed correctly, the filing that must be done on time, and the cleanup that is necessary to meet government regulations.

Parent Tip 73

If your child has a neurological condition such as ADHD, Asperger's, or a learning disability, get in touch with the counselor who works with students with disabilities at the college as soon as you apply. Different laws govern colleges and high schools when it comes to accommodations for students with special needs. You need to make sure your expectations of services are in line with the services the college is required to provide.

Parent Tip 74

Half of all colleges that grant bachelor's degrees fail to graduate even 50 percent of students who enroll in college freshman year. This suggests that many schools are more focused on getting students in the door than on supporting them once they are on campus. It also suggests that many students don't find the right college to begin with or are unprepared to be successful at the institution they choose.

As a parent, two of the questions you should ask college recruiters are "What is your graduation rate?" and "How many of your first-year students graduate from your institution within six years?"

In addition, if your child needs remedial courses in math, writing, or reading, you need to check out the quality of the academic support services that will be available to your child on campus. A student who scores into remedial classes is academically vulnerable when going off to college. Make sure that whatever school you and your child select has the support systems your child will need and that your child knows how to access those support systems.

Parent Tip 75

High school students who are good at math are routinely encouraged to consider engineering as a career. But if a student finds the three semesters of college calculus needed for an engineering degree too daunting, there are other engineering careers to consider that require fewer math courses.

At the four-year level, there are two engineering-related bachelor's degrees: engineering and engineering technology. Many community colleges also offer a two-year degree in engineering technology that can be woven into a bachelor's degree in engineering technology later on.

Engineers and engineering technologists work in partnership on projects in a variety of industries, including architecture, construction, energy, telecommunications, health care, information technology, and manufacturing. Your child can research the differences in these roles by using the Occupational Outlook Handbook and by doing informational interviews with people working in engineering firms.

Not all four-year colleges and universities offer both engineering and engineering technology degrees. In addition, the engineering technology degree may not be offered at the same campus as the engineering degree. Many states divide funding for technical degrees between different institutions within the state to save money. Not all campuses within a state system will have all majors. It is important to know the degree options available at the schools you are considering, which you can do by checking out the degrees, programs, and majors on the college Web site.

Parent Tip 76

One standard measure of success for K–12 school districts is how many graduates go on to college after high school. Since less than 50 percent of all students who enroll in college graduate from college, a good question for K–12 parents to ask is how many of a district's students who go to college eventually graduate.

You need to have a realistic assessment of your child's preparedness for college. This means assessing the rigor of your child's high school. One indicator of this is the track record of other students in the high school your child attends. Talk to your high school guidance counselor to get information on the college success of recent graduates of your high school.

Parent Tip 77

Make sure you are not paying twice for a college course your child took in high school.

A dual-credit class in U.S. History can have the same course equivalency as an Advanced Placement course in U.S. History, a CLEP test in U.S. History, and a U.S. History class taken once your child is in college. Since students in many high schools are offered the opportunity to take college classes in a variety of formats, it is important to make sure you are not duplicating college credit.

Colleges have transfer equivalency pages on their Web sites that will give you information about how classes taken in high school will transfer. Find out the college's policy on AP, CLEP, and dual-credit courses. Many schools have a limit on how many credits they will accept for courses completed in high school. Make sure you have transcripts from colleges providing dual credit and from outside test credentialing organizations sent to the colleges your student will be attending before your child enrolls in first-year classes. Also confirm that your child is properly enrolled in the dual-credit course in high school. Dual-credit courses often have an additional enrollment form or fee for the college that awards the credit. If the form is not completed or the fee not paid, college credit will not be earned.

Parent Tip 78

If your child is taking AP and dual-credit classes in high school in order to reduce time and money spent on college, verify with college recruiters that your child will be able to enroll in the sophomore-level classes she needs when she is enrolling as a freshman.

Many colleges and universities enroll students according to grade level: seniors enroll first, juniors next, sophomores next, and incoming freshmen last. This method exists so that students already in the pipeline for a major can get the courses they need to complete a degree.

If your child has completed 30 hours of general education in high school, plans on majoring in business, and needs to take financial accounting as a freshman, will there be openings in that class by the time she is allowed to enroll? If not, your child will be taking other courses freshman year that may or may not apply to her degree.

CHAPTER 10

Taking a Different Path

If your child is not interested in a four-year college degree, he's not doomed to flipping burgers the rest of his life. However, you and he will have to be resourceful in uncovering alternative career paths that exist in today's economy.

Lost in the Middle

Young people in the middle or lower half of their high school class often have a difficult transition to college. This is because they have the expectation of attending college without the academic preparation to be successful in college.

Consider Daniel:

Daniel hated high school and enrolled in the local community college after graduation. He told his academic advisor, "I just need 12 hours to stay on my parents' health insurance."

Daniel wanted to take "just the basics" so he could transfer "somewhere" as soon as possible. He was a C student in high school, where he took the high school diploma curriculum, which required fewer math credits than his other diploma options, which were a college-prep diploma, an honors diploma, and an International Baccalaureate diploma.

In his senior year of high school, Daniel attended classes for two hours each morning. Then he went to work at his "internship" at an auto parts store, where he worked 30 hours a week as a sales associate. His boss completed paperwork each semester to meet the internship requirement for the high school, but beyond the paperwork, there was no additional training or mentoring as part of Daniel's "work-study" job.

Once admitted to the local community college, Daniel was surprised and irritated to learn he had to take, and pay for, 12 hours of remedial courses before he could begin the college-level courses that would count towards his degree. Based on his placement scores at the community college, Daniel had 9th-grade math skills (he had taken Algebra I, Geometry, and Algebra II in high school, but got a D in Algebra II) and was reading at the 10.5 grade level. He was enrolled in 12 hours his first semester at the community college and continued to work 30 or more hours at the auto parts store. Daniel felt he could not work fewer hours because of his car expenses. He was eager to get out of the house but saw no way he could afford an apartment of his own.

The odds are very great that Daniel will leave college after a few semesters without a degree or career certificate. He will settle on the lower rungs of the economic ladder because he has no specialized skills or work experience to do anything else. Daniel will be left behind in college.

One of the facts not shared by college recruiters is that only 47 percent of all students who start college ever finish a college degree or complete a two-year transfer program. Graduation and transfer rates are as low as 25 percent at some community colleges.

Forty years ago, Daniel's lack of preparation wouldn't have mattered. Daniel would have been "tracked" during high school and placed in a vocational technical program that did not demand rigorous academic preparation. He would have graduated from high school and found a well-paying manufacturing job in his community.

In the past 25 years, large numbers of those high-pay/low-skill manufacturing jobs disappeared. Few high-pay/low-skill jobs came along to replace them. As a result, many young people like Daniel see no other option than to enroll in a community college and hope for the best. Because most community colleges are open-admissions institutions, students like Daniel can be admitted to college without regard to their academic qualifications. They are required, however, to take placement tests to determine whether they can start with college-level courses or must take, and pay for, remedial courses first.

Daniel lacks career maturity. No one has ever helped him shape a realistic career goal or connect his high school efforts to the adult lifestyle he desires. No one has educated him about the job market.

If you are the parent of a young person like Daniel, you need to be a parent advocate just as much as if your child were in Advanced Placement classes. You need to get involved. Help your child identify other options besides a four-year college degree. You need to figure out how your child can get training for one of the many technician-level jobs in today's economy.

Looking at the Structure of the Job Market

To understand the role of technician-level jobs in the economy, look at the Bureau of Labor Statistics information in Chapter 3, Chart 2, another way.

Jobs in the economy can be divided into three broad levels of employment: professional, technician, and operative.

Professional Jobs

Professional jobs are those requiring a bachelor's degree or higher. Approximately 21 percent of all U.S. jobs are professional jobs. These include doctor, lawyer, accountant, teacher, engineer, business manager, and so on. Professional jobs are the ones most commonly identified as career goals by high school students and their parents.

Technician Jobs

Technician jobs are those requiring long-term on-the-job training, vocational/technical certification, or an associate degree for employment. Approximately 27 percent of all jobs require this level of postsecondary training. Electrician, plumber, computer-aided-drafting technician, nurse, engineering technician, radiological technician, EKG technician, home health aide, and medical assistant are all examples of technician-level jobs.

Operative Jobs

Finally, there are operative jobs. Retail sales associates, fast-food restaurant managers, meat-processing factory workers, and housekeepers are all operative jobs, which are defined as those jobs requiring only short-term to moderate-term on-the-job training. The majority of jobs in the U.S. economy—52 percent—are operative jobs.

Identifying Alternatives to a Four-Year Degree

Studies show that more than 59 percent of teenagers, including Daniel, intend to have a professional job. But if Daniel stays on his current path—attending college when he is unmotivated and unprepared—the odds are great that he will not end up in a professional level job. He will likely drop out of college and continue working at his operative-level job at the auto parts store, possibly advancing to a job requiring moderate-term on-the-job training, such as assistant store manager. Many front-line management jobs in retail sales require moderate-term on-the-job training.

If Daniel realizes that a four-year college degree may not be his best choice, he can identify other options. In skills language, Daniel can learn specific-content skills that will pay better than his current specific-content skills, which include selling auto parts, taking customer orders, and inventorying auto supplies. Daniel can get additional training to learn better-paying skills that are in demand in today's economy.

There are a number of ways he can do this:

1. Daniel can enroll in a technical program offered through his high school while he is still a high school student.

   As states and local communities have become aware of projected skills shortages when boomer-era workers retire, they have invested time and money in upgrading the career-technical programs offered through high schools. These new career-technical programs are more academically rigorous than the old "vo-tech" or "tech prep" programs of 30 years ago. Many of the new career programs develop strong academic skills, particularly in the STEM subjects of science, engineering, technology, and math, while at the same time providing state-of-the-art training for entry-level jobs in health care, engineering technology, electronics, hospitality, and personal services. Increasingly these programs are aligned with more advanced education provided by area career centers and community colleges.

2. Daniel can look into apprenticeships and other long-term on-the job training programs.

   Union and non-union apprenticeships prepare students for careers as electricians, pipe fitters, carpenters, glaziers, plumbers, sheet metal workers, and other trades jobs.

The best way to find out how to get into these apprenticeship programs is networking. Find someone who is working in a local apprenticeship-based job and have your child do an informational interview with that person. You can also do a simple Internet search for apprenticeships in your city or state or contact a local union hall to find how to get into an apprenticeship program in your community.

3. Daniel can join the military and learn an entry-level job there.

   There are over 4,000 different military jobs. These jobs teach specific-content skills that can be used in non-military jobs later on. In addition, many of the same life skills young people develop living away from home in a college setting are developed living away from home in the military. Young people learn to value diversity, share living quarters with people of different backgrounds, manage time and money, work with people in positions of authority, and set personal boundaries in unregulated social situations. Military benefits offer a way for young people who cannot afford to go to college after high school to attend college while they are in the military and after they are out.

4. Daniel can check out jobs requiring work experience in a related occupation.

   These jobs include first-line supervisors of mechanics, installers, and repairers, as well as many specialized transportation and industrial jobs. To get these jobs, your child would need to work as an entry-level mechanic, installer, or repairer to qualify for a better-paying job within the industry. Training for entry-level positions may be offered by a local career center or community college or through on-the-job training. Your child will have opportunities to move up into well-paying supervisory positions.

5. Daniel can investigate hidden on-the-job training opportunities within an organization or industry that interests him.

   Some organizations have in-house training programs open only to current employees of the organization. An example would be a histology-technician training program run by a local hospital. This training program is open only to current hospital employees who have completed a college course in both chemistry and biology.

6. Daniel can consider getting a postsecondary vocational certificate or award.

These programs train students for jobs such as cosmetologists, certified nursing assistants, chefs, surgical technologists, and refrigeration technicians. Training for these careers is offered by regional career centers, proprietary schools, technical institutes, and community colleges.

7. Daniel can redirect his community college studies from a transfer degree to an associate degree in a career field.

   Career and technical associate degrees prepare students for jobs such as nurses, radiological technicians, engineering technicians, industrial-maintenance technicians, environmental health and safety technicians, and computer-support technicians. To get into the academic program for the most popular associate degree career programs, such as nursing or radiology, your child will have to compete academically with other applicants. While there is a strong demand for graduates in these areas, the training programs for these careers are expensive to run and admit only a limited number of students each year. Your child will need to have strong basic academic skills and demonstrate success in college-level prerequisite courses to be admitted to these programs.

When choosing one of the postsecondary options described in this list, here are some additional things to consider:

- For some careers, there is a clear academic ladder from one level to the next. For other careers, there is not.

  A licensed professional nurse can "bridge" into an associate degree nursing program and later bridge into a Bachelor of Science nursing program, thereby moving up professionally to greater levels of responsibility and income. A drafting technician with an Associate of Applied Science degree in computer-aided drafting and design can bridge to a Bachelor of Science degree in technology offered by a state university with baccalaureate degrees in technology areas.

  Other educational paths are terminal career paths. A pharmacy technician job is not the first step to becoming a pharmacist. A physical therapy assistant job is not the first step toward becoming a physical therapist.

  Talk to someone currently employed in the field to identify the educational bridges within a career.

- Postsecondary programs differ in cost and in credentialing.

  Career centers and community colleges are publicly supported. Proprietary schools and institutes are often for-profit institutions. Since career centers and proprietary institutions sometimes have different credentialing boards than colleges and universities, credits earned at one institution may or may not transfer easily to another institution.

  It is important for your child do his research. Have him talk to graduates of any vocational programs he is considering to see how it worked out for them, both in the job market and in moving up with higher education.

- Going a career/technical route after high school doesn't eliminate the possibility of your child earning a bachelor's degree later on.

  More and more colleges and universities are working to develop educational pathways for students to move up from an associate degree in a technical area to a higher-level bachelor's degree in technology or business. In the meantime, a post-secondary career program can buy your child time to gain career maturity. It can enable your child to get into the workplace, start earning money, and get established in an industry before jumping into a four-year degree.

But what if your high school student is not your main concern? What if you are worried about a young person who is out of college and can't find a job? What are some things you can do to help?

Parent Tip 79

In researching technician-level educational opportunities, the same caution applies as for researching majors at the four-year level: Just because there is a degree or certificate in the field doesn't mean there are well-paying jobs in the field.

Some vocational training programs are worth more in the marketplace than others. Just because a program is offered at an educational institution that is covered by federal financial aid doesn't mean that there is a demand for graduates of the program or that those graduates did well in the job market. It is up to your child to check this out before committing time and money to any postsecondary educational program. Find a person who graduated from the program and have your child talk to that person.

Parent Tip 80

You may have a distorted picture of the job market if you are only looking at the economy through the lens of your own organization.

Some work environments have more professional jobs than technician jobs. In K–12 education, many people have bachelor's degrees and higher. Educators earn pay increases by earning college credit hours beyond those required for a bachelor's degree. In the hospitality industry, many workers have only short-term or moderate-term on-the-job training. Advancement on the pay scale is based on job performance rather than educational credential.

Look around your own company or organization. Identify the three job levels in play. Which are the professional jobs? Which are the technician jobs? Which are the operative jobs? What education and work experience is needed to perform each level of job?

Parent Tip 81

If your child is unmotivated or insecure about attending college, consider letting her take a gap year after high school.

The practice of a gap year originated in Europe, where young adults are given the option of taking a year off after high school or college to travel, work, or volunteer in other countries.

A gap year before entering college in the United States is rare. Most students enroll in college right out of high school. Many U.S. parents are reluctant to support a gap year. They fear that if their child takes time off, she will never go back to college. They worry that their child will lose health-care coverage if she is not enrolled in college full time.

But it can be very expensive in the long run to force an unmotivated student to go to college on your parental timetable. A transcript full of failed coursework will add thousands of dollars to your total college costs once your child goes back to school and has to repeat the failed courses. In addition, your child may be denied admission to the college of her choice because of her previous college record.

A good alternative might be a gap year. This could be the experience your child needs to develop the motivation to go to college.

The key to a successful gap year is having clear expectations about what is to be accomplished during the time off. What will your child be doing if she is not in school? Will she be traveling? If so, how will she pay for it? Will she be doing volunteer work? Will she have a job? If so, will she be paying part of her rent and living expenses while she is not in school?

Set clear boundaries up front to ensure a positive gap year experience.

Parent Tip 82

Chances are you remember high school as being divided into two groups of students—the school leaders who were good at academics, sports, and extra-curricular activities and everybody else. The school leaders were channeled into a rigorous college-prep curriculum that prepared them to go on to college and professional and managerial jobs and everybody else got routed into "vo-tech."

This two-tiered high school structure mirrored the Old Economy in which there were managers, who had the answers and gave directions, and workers, who did what they were told.

The economy has changed. Management ranks have been flattened, and many rote jobs have been eliminated by technology. The well-paying, non-management jobs in the New Economy require more complex skills on the part of workers, who must now demonstrate technical expertise as well as strong skills in reading comprehension, writing, and math to get ahead.

Some high schools have begun to address this shift in the economy with innovative career-technical programs. High schools, area career centers, community colleges, and four-year institutions are increasingly working together to develop a variety of routes for students besides going to college without adequate academic preparation and jumping into the 40 hours of general education courses that are the foundation of a liberal arts degree.

Check out what is going on in your high school. If you are fortunate to be in a school district that is directing resources to improving career-technical programming, your child could learn the skills for an entry-level job in a technical or health-care area while in high school and still have the academic skills to go on for more education if needed or desired.

Parent Tip 83

Many parents are reluctant to encourage a child to pursue a technical program while in high school because they fear that people with four-year-college degrees will take all the "good" jobs in the future.

(continued)

(continued)

The reality is that college graduates will not take jobs from workers with specialized skills that are in demand. Job openings are a function of the demand for goods and services. A person with a bachelor's degree in psychology and work experience in retail sales will not take the job of a computer technician with industry certification in network security.

Carefully examine your beliefs about the job market, especially any sweeping assumptions you are making about "all jobs in the future." The job market is much more complex and fluid than most people assume. There are many more paths from one level of occupational training to the next than when you were in high school. Check them out. Technical training in high school is no longer a "dead end" in many communities.

Parent Tip 84

Even if your child is not planning on joining the military, she can make use of the career and educational planning resources developed by the military, including the Armed Services Vocational Aptitude Battery (ASVAB) and the March 2 Success Web site.

The ASVAB is a timed, multi-aptitude test that measures your child's arithmetic reasoning, word knowledge, paragraph comprehension, and mathematical knowledge. The ASVAB is administered in high schools, and the scores are given to students, along with an access code that allows them to use their scores to explore careers and learn about the pathways to various occupations through the ASVAB Career Exploration Program Web site.

March 2 Success is a free online test preparation Web site to help students improve their performance on math, science, and English tests, as well as on the ACT and SAT tests. March 2 Success also provides diagnostic tests to help students identify their strengths and weaknesses. Based on the results of the test, a customized program of instruction can be built that focuses attention on those academic areas that need improvement.

To find out about the ASVAB, contact your high school counselor. To find out about March 2 Success, check it out online at www.march2success.com and see if it is something that could benefit your child.

Parent Tip 85

If you are the parent of a "middle-skills" student—a B and C student in high school who is not taking honors classes and who is not particularly engaged in academics—you need to be proactive. Insist that your child keep studying English and math all four years of high school, as well as develop a game plan for life after high school graduation.

One way to do this is to investigate the Career Pathways programming in your school district.

Career Pathways is a workforce development strategy focused on helping people transition from education to the workforce. At the high school level, it includes curriculum offerings designed to help students develop their academic skills in reading, writing, and math by connecting them to real-world applications in various careers. Career Pathways is organized around the 16 career clusters identified by the U.S. government as the main industry and service areas of the economy. Here are the career clusters:

1. Agriculture, Food, and Natural Resources
2. Architecture and Construction
3. Arts, Audio/Visual Technology, and Communications
4. Business, Management, and Administration
5. Education and Training
6. Finance
7. Government and Public Administration
8. Health Science
9. Hospitality and Tourism
10. Human Services
11. Information Technology
12. Public Safety, Corrections, and Security
13. Manufacturing
14. Marketing, Sales, and Service
15. Science, Technology, Engineering, and Mathematics
16. Transportation, Distribution, and Logistics

Some parents and educators are reluctant to support Career Pathways programming because they believe it forces students to choose a career path before they are ready. In reality, a good Career Pathways program develops college-ready

(continued)

(continued)

transferable skills in reading, writing, science, and math through career course content. It engages students in their academics by connecting those academics to real-world career applications. The goal of Career Pathways is to ensure that more students have college-ready transferable skills upon high school graduation. They can choose to follow that career path or a different one when they are in college. Without college-ready skills, however, students will have limited options.

All jobs, no matter their required level of education, are in one of these 16 areas of the economy. Career Pathways educates students about the different areas of the economy, the levels of jobs within industries, and the variety of pathways to employment in different career fields. It attempts to break down the two-track system of high school education in which students are divided into college-bound and vocational students. It teaches students life skills along with academic skills.

Many people underestimate the level of math and communication skills all students, not just the college bound, will need to be successful in 21st century jobs. Middle-skills students fall through the cracks in many high schools. They don't drop out of high school; they go to a community college and drop out there. Career Pathways programming tries to ensure that all students have the academic skills to continue their education after high school, as well have some idea of where they might like to work after they complete college or technical training.

CHAPTER 11

Moving On from College

If you have a child who is out of college but floundering around, the first thing you need to do is discourage him from going to graduate school immediately to solve the problem. Even though the word on the street is that a master's degree is the new bachelor's degree, most young people need to figure out an initial career path and get some entry-level work experience before signing on for more student loan debt.

To understand this, step back and look at the career-planning process in general. Figure 1 shows you the career-planning cycle.

Any job search or career transition always begins at the same place—a self-assessment of the skills, interests, and values of the job seeker (at the left side of Figure 1).

It doesn't matter what the transition is about—finding a first job right out of college, regrouping after a layoff due to downsizing or corporate merger, or re-entering the workplace after raising children—the starting point is always the same: self-assessment. The job seeker can then use that self-assessment information to identify jobs in the economy that fit with his skills, interests, and values.

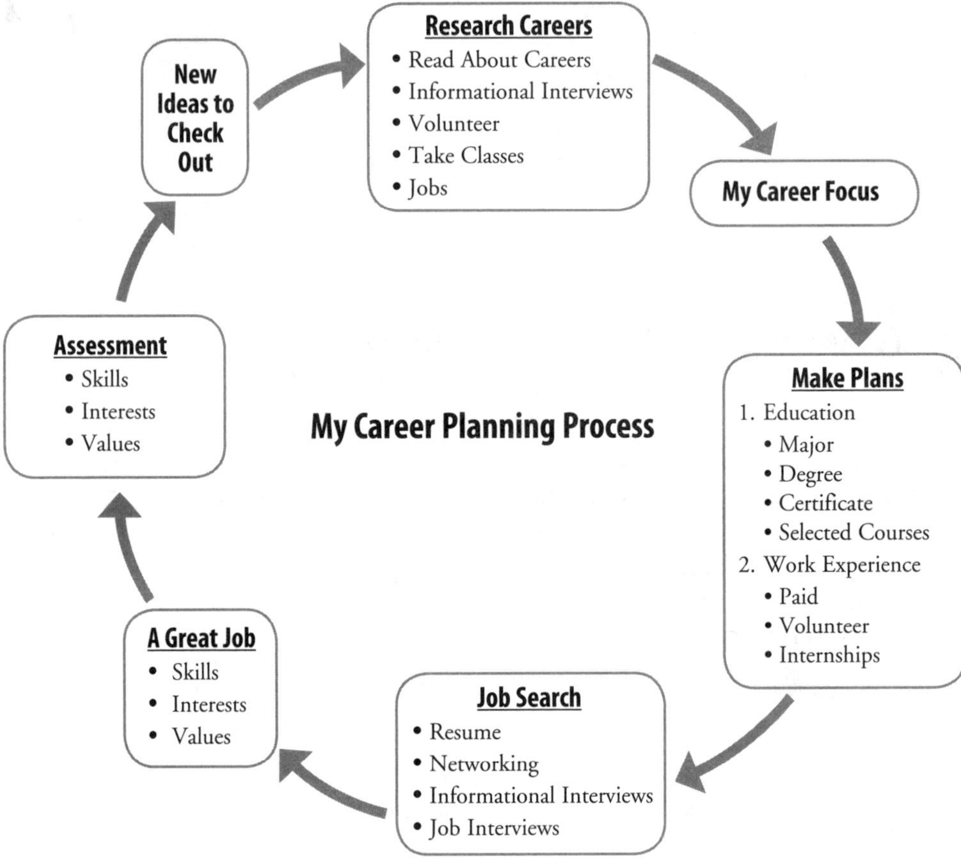

Figure 1: The career-planning cycle.

Going Back to Step 1

If your child is out of college but unfocused, he needs to answer four career-planning questions:

1. What skills do I enjoy using?
2. Where are those skills used in the economy?
3. Which of those jobs fits with my values and personality preferences?
4. What additional education or work experience would I need to get the job I really want?

Until your child has answered these questions, graduate school is premature.

This is not what many young people and their parents want to hear. A bachelor's degree now involves a family economic outlay of $50,000 to $150,000. Many graduates start their work lives with significant amounts of student loan debt. No young person wants to hear he has to start at the bottom of the ladder after investing that much money in a bachelor's degree.

If your child has a high-demand, high-pay skill set, as represented by a bachelor's degree in engineering or accounting, the bottom of the ladder may be a job paying $60,000 a year with benefits. If your child has a low-demand or low-pay skill set, as represented by a bachelor's degree in English or art history, the bottom of the ladder may be a job paying $28,000 a year without benefits.

Faced with this reality, your child may conclude that a master's degree is the missing piece to his career puzzle. He will be vulnerable to the Internet advertising of hundreds of colleges and universities now offering master's degree programs on campus and online. This advertising tells him he will never get ahead without a master's degree.

But there is a right time and a wrong time for graduate school. Adding more education at the graduate school level without doing the self-assessment and research necessary to identify a meaningful career goal is simply doing the same thing and expecting different results. In 2008, 862,900 people holding master's degrees and 206,100 people holding doctoral or professional degrees were working in jobs that required only short-term on-the-job training. Out of college and unhappy at work, your child needs to determine if the problem is lack of education, lack of work experience, or lack of focus before going back to school.

Consider Jenny's experience:

Jenny graduated from college four years ago with a bachelor's degree in communication studies. She attended a mid-sized state university located two and a half hours away from her home. During the academic year, she worked on campus as a residence-hall assistant and as a college-admissions aide, coordinating mailings to prospective students and giving campus tours.

During her junior year in college, Jenny went to the campus career center to get help finding an internship. She had decided she wanted a career in public relations, and she knew she would need work experience along with her degree to find a PR job after graduation. She thought an internship would be a good move.

She interviewed for and received an internship at large PR firm in her home city. The summer after her junior year she worked full time at the PR firm for minimum wage. She found she hated the job and wanted no part of the high-pressure corporate public relations business.

Jenny finished college and moved back home. Her mom suggested that Jenny go on and get her MBA since Jenny wasn't sure what she wanted to do. Jenny said she was burned out on school and wanted to work first. She brainstormed options with her parents.

Her dad suggested she meet with a friend of his who owned a small management-consulting company. This man offered Jenny a full-time marketing job without benefits. Her job was to upgrade the company's marketing and promotional materials, organize the company's workshops, and maintain the company Web site. Jenny's parents purchased a high-deductible, major-medical health insurance plan to cover Jenny until she was able to pay for health insurance on her own.

Jenny enjoyed her new job. She found it used her communication, project-management, and organizational skills. She could not, however, afford to move out of her parents' house on the income from her full-time job. She decided to take a weekend job as a waitress to earn enough money to move into an apartment with three friends.

One day, while coordinating a workshop for the consultant, Jenny began talking to one of the executives at a company that provided medical-records software to hospitals. This software company had experienced tremendous growth in the past five years. The executive was impressed with Jenny and encouraged her to apply for a job with his company.

Jenny was hired as a consultant. Her job was to coordinate projects with clients who were converting to her company's software. She traveled four days a week, providing on-site training and support to health-care organizations transitioning to her company's system.

Jenny found she enjoyed using her communication and problem-solving skills in the health-care environment. She also liked the salary and benefit package provided by her mid-sized company. She found she enjoyed working with health-care administrators, and she seemed to understand the issues they were facing. After networking with several of her contacts in the health-care industry, including the chief operating officer of a major health-care system, Jenny decided to go back to graduate school for a master's degree in health-care administration. She felt confident her work experience and contacts in health care would make her marketable as a health-care business analyst after she earned her graduate degree.

Jenny found her career path in the health-care sector of the economy. It is not the career path she or her parents would have predicted when Jenny graduated from college with a bachelor's degree in communication studies. By gaining exposure to several jobs, Jenny identified her best skills, which were communication, strategic thinking, and organizing systems. She clarified some of her life values, which were making a difference in people's lives and improving the health-care system. At the same time, she identified a path that promised to satisfy her work values, which included opportunities for advancement, a good benefit package, and employability in the future.

If your child is considering going to graduate school, he may have skipped to the Make Plans area of Figure 1. If so, he needs to go back and complete the Assessment and Research Careers steps before making educational plans. While it is tempting to believe that even though a master's degree isn't required for a job, having one will move your child ahead of other candidates, this is an assumption, not a fact.

If your child has little work experience and a bachelor's degree, adding more education at the master's level may not be the best move. For many employers, education is considered theory, while work experience is considered proof that the person can deliver real-world results. Employers want both.

According to Bureau of Labor Statistics data (see Chapter 3, Chart 3), less than 5 percent of jobs in the United States require a master's degree or higher. Without doing the work of self-assessment and career research, your child runs the risk of going into more debt and still not landing a good job. A better move may be getting targeted entry-level work experience rather than earning another degree.

Helping a College Graduate Regroup

How can you help facilitate a productive discussion with your child around these sensitive issues?

First, sit down with your child and discuss the career-planning process in Figure 1. Encourage him to do the self-assessment exercises outlined in Chapters 4 and 5 of this book. Have him contact career services at his college or university to access assessment resources or go to a local community college and get help there.

Networking for Ideas

Next, help your child identify his network. Even if your child is floundering around in the job market, some of his friends aren't. Using the My Network worksheet in Chapter 3, have your child identify the connections he already has. These friends are networking contacts that can provide job leads and information-interview contacts. He also can do preliminary research on industries and organizations that interest him by using the Company/Industry Research worksheet.

COMPANY/INDUSTRY RESEARCH

By learning more about a company or industry, you can focus your interests and determine future goals. Information can be acquired from the company Web site, from Internet articles about the company and industry, and through networking with people who work for the company or in the industry.

Here are some questions to research online:

- What is a general description of the company/industry?
- What products/services does it provide?
- What is the financial history and status of the company? Its future outlook?
- Where are the headquarters? Where are the branch offices?
- What are the categories of positions of the people employed?
- What are the current job opportunities in this business?
- What skills are needed to work in this company or industry?
- What are the mission, values, and vision of the company?

Here are some additional questions to ask of someone who is working for a company of interest to you:

- What are the cultural characteristics of this company or industry?
- How does your company compare to others in the industry? How do they compete?
- What are the trends and developments that influence this company/organization?
- What are the global implications for this industry or company?
- What are the problems facing this company?

- How do the pay scale and benefits compare to other companies in the same industry?
- What kind of training is provided to employees?
- How would I fit into this business or industry?

Your child's network can provide your child with

- Introductions to people in various sectors of the economy, including health care, business and marketing, hospitality, construction and manufacturing, retail, communications, finance and insurance, transportation, and so on.
- Insight into what employers are looking for in candidates.
- Suggestions on how to redo his resume to target a better job.
- Job leads.
- Additional networking contacts.

Identifying Your Values

Next, open up a conversation with your child about values as they relate to career satisfaction. As you can see from the career-planning process, part of finding meaningful work involves identifying your values.

Values drive career decisions. Values are how people evaluate the merits or drawbacks of different jobs. Values are what make people say "I'll take the job!" or "There is no way I would do that for a living!"

People make career decisions based on their own unique hierarchy of values. Your hierarchy of values may or may not be the same as your child's. Two values checklists will help you and your child think about values. One is called "Work Values," and the other is called "Life Values." People make career decisions according to how they prioritize both.

Work values are criteria that impact the day-to-day experience of a job. Work values include the hours, the type of boss, the salary, and the working conditions. The Work Values sidebar gives a sample of work values important to many people. Work values are on a continuum in that people assign varying degrees of importance to each individual work value as a part of their job satisfaction. In addition, as a parent, you probably have a much clearer idea of your work values than your child does because you have been in the workforce before and have held a variety of jobs since high school. Because you have more work experience to draw on in articulating your work values, you need to be careful not to overwhelm your child with your experience and opinions. Let your child explore work values for himself by getting more exposure to different work environments through informational interviewing.

Work Values	
Mimimum salary needed: $	Maximum salary desired: $
Employer-paid health insurance	Pay for my own health insurance
Work with little supervision	Work with close supervision
Receive frequent feedback	Receive little feedback on my work
Short commute to work	Don't mind commuting to work
Maximum of 40 hours a week	Don't mind working overtime
Work indoors	Work outside
Fast-paced work	Slow-paced work
Public contact	Little public contact
Physical activity	Stay mostly in one place
Regular schedule	Flexible schedule
Safe work environment	OK working in hazardous conditions
Work alone	Work with other people
Job security	No problem changing jobs
Repetitive work tasks	Variety of work tasks
Opportunities for promotion	Like being a worker bee
Feel valued as an employee	Don't need affirmation on the job

Work Values

Work for large company	Work for small company
Travel is part of the job	No travel involved in my job
Short education/training time	Long training time
Perform one task at a time	Do many things at once
Work in an orderly environment	OK in a disorganized work area
Work with people I enjoy	Co-worker relationships not important
Work in a pleasant environment	Surroundings not important

Life values are broader values about helping people, making lots of money, making a difference in the world, or being recognized as the leader of the group. The Life Values sidebar shows some life values important to many people and their definitions. Have your child rank their importance in the Priority column.

Life Values

Life Value	Definition	Priority
Making lots of money	The dollar amount I want to make is $	
Prestige	Being well known and well respected in my field	
Independence	Freedom to do my work in my own way	
Directly helping other people	My work has a direct, positive impact on people's lives	

(continued)

(continued)

Life Values

Life Value	Definition	Priority
Competition	Compete against others to achieve individual or team goals	
Competence	Feel confident I know what I am doing	
Recognition	Receive recognition from others for my work	
Responsibility for others	Have responsibility for meeting the needs of other people	
Authority over others	Have authority to direct the actions of other people	
Achievement	Be able to set goals and meet them	
Intellectual challenge	Learn new and difficult things	
Having fun	Have fun on the job	
Low stress	Little pressure on my job	
Lifestyle	Balance career and home activities; time for outside interests	
Creativity	Develop new ideas, products, and processes	
Security	Have a job that is stable and not subject to layoffs	

Life Values		
Life Value	**Definition**	**Priority**
Advancement	Have opportunities for promotion	
Autonomy	Be my own boss	
Power	Have control over people, decision making, and resources	
Variety	Change work activities and projects often	

Most young people in college have some idea of their life values. They know if it is important to them to be helping other people, making a lot of money, or achieving recognition in a field.

Few young people in college have a very clear understanding of their work values. This is because they have little exposure to the world of work.

One of the key work values for most adults is making enough money to pay for the lifestyle they want to enjoy. Few young people know what this work value means to them until they are fully self-supporting. Many young people in college have little understanding of how much money it takes to pay the bills. It is only when they are out of college and living on their own that the relation of salary to lifestyle becomes real. It is only then that they begin to make real-life tradeoffs that color the career decisions of working adults. These are all things to discuss with your child when he is looking for work.

Evaluating Grad School as an Option

Finally, if, after doing self-assessment and researching opportunities in a field, your child still wants to go to graduate school, here is a list of things he should consider as part of doing a reality check on his grad school plans:

1. Separate the degree from the subject area or discipline. All master's degrees are not equal. Some subject areas are worth more in the job market than others. A master's degree in athletic training will play out

differently, in terms of salary and employment opportunities, than a master's degree in speech-language pathology.

2. Understand that a master's degree is preparation for a career. Every career is subject to laws of supply and demand. Before you start any graduate program, talk to three people who have the master's degree you are considering. These people need to be working in the field full-time. Ask them these questions:

   - What is the job market like?
   - What is the starting salary?
   - Are most jobs full or part time?
   - How hard is it to advance in the field?
   - How are technology, globalization, and managed care impacting the demand for people with this degree?
   - Is getting this particular master's degree my best career move at this time?

3. Recognize that while some jobs are strictly degree oriented, particularly jobs in health care, education, and social services, most jobs require relevant work experience, as well as a degree, for advancement. When your level of education is out of balance with your work experience, you may have trouble moving ahead. Instead of going to graduate school, and going into debt to finance it, consider whether your best career move is to decide where you want to start in the economy and begin building work experience from there. Once you have relevant work experience and a clear career focus, you will know what additional education you need to get ahead. And if you're lucky, you'll be working for an employer who will help you pay for it.

Now that you have helped your child with career planning, is there any way you could have used this information to help your child get out of college in just four years?

Parent Tip 86

A career doesn't have to be the complete outlet for one's interests, personality, and skills.

It is unrealistic for most students to expect their first job out of college to be a "dream job." Discussion about skills, interests, and values can help your child see that a career is only one piece of a complex puzzle that fits together to make a satisfying life.

While it is important to find interesting paid employment, it is equally important to know how to fill in the gaps by finding creative outlets for important interests and skills in other places besides paid employment. This is career/life balance.

Parent Tip 87

Just as a business major is often the default value for undecided students and their parents at the undergraduate level, a law degree or MBA is often the default value for undecided students and their parents at the graduate-school level. It is just as important for your child to research the economic realities for graduate education as it is for undergraduate education. How much can your child realistically expect to make starting out?

The median salary of law school graduates nine months after graduation was $60,000 in 2005. The median income for all lawyers in 2006 was $102,470, with the middle half of all lawyers making between $70,000 and $145,000 per year. What will be the relationship between your child's salary, in both the short and the long term, to her student loan debt for law school?

As a graduate-school student, your child will be eligible to borrow as much as $138,500 in federally funded student loans. If she borrows that amount, she will be facing a monthly payment of approximately $1,600 a month for 10 years or $961 a month for 25 years. According to the 8 percent rule, your child would need to be making a salary of approximately $239,000 a year to afford a 10-year loan of $138,500 for graduate school and $144,000 a year to afford a 25-year loan. What impact will this debt have on your child's lifestyle once she is out of school?

Parent Tip 88

As more and more undergraduates emerge from college burdened with student loan debt, it is very tempting for them to see graduate school as a way to defer payment on their existing student loans and, at the same time, escape a current job they do not like. After all, the wages of bachelor's-degreed workers have stayed flat in recent years while the wages of master's-degreed workers have increased. A graduate student is eligible to borrow much more money in federal student loans than an undergraduate. And relentless advertising over the Internet by colleges trying to capitalize on student fears about the economy has convinced many young people that they will be left behind if they don't have a master's degree or higher.

(continued)

(continued)

The fact is, if every young adult who currently holds a bachelor's degree went on to earn a master's degree, there would still be only 1.7 percent of U.S. jobs that require a master's degree. Another 1.3 percent of jobs require a professional degree in a field such as medicine or law, and another 1.4 percent of jobs require a Ph.D. This is a total of approximately 4.4 percent of all jobs that require a master's degree or higher.

Unless your child is willing to take on more student loan debt for graduate school only to emerge underemployed, he needs to be strategic about getting a master's degree. He should not assume that a master's degree will guarantee career advancement, particularly if he has no significant work experience. He needs to carefully consider the cost/benefit ratio and the timing of graduate school. He needs to get first-hand information from people holding the degree he is considering before making the decision to go on to graduate school.

Parent Tip 89

What happens when a journalism major no longer wants to work in the field?

This question is on the mind of many young adults who earned a degree in a specific career field, such as journalism, only to find the industry they had entered in the midst of structural economic change or downsizing due to the recession. In recent years, several newspapers that had been in print over 100 years ceased publication, highlighting the instability of the job market for journalism graduates in their 20s and early 30s. Traditional print and broadcasting jobs are disappearing, and the "new media" jobs that are replacing them require different skills. Some young adults just a few years out of college already want to "re-career."

This can be a discouraging and demoralizing situation for both young people and their parents. These young adults conscientiously earned a degree in a specific career area with the expectation that it would pay off financially and provide job satisfaction and job security. They now see themselves as having limited skills. They need help identifying their transferable skills and learning how to network to find different ways to use their skills in the job market.

A journalism degree, like an education or interior design degree, develops career-specific skills. When a young person no longer wants to use those career-specific skills in the field, that degree becomes a transferable skills degree in the job market. This means that the journalism or education degree, like a communication studies or history degree, now represents transferable skills to an employer rather than specific-content skills. It is up to the young person to figure out where to apply his or her transferable skills in the job market and get relevant work experience.

Career and alumni services at your child's former college or university can be an excellent place to start the regrouping process. Encourage your child to contact career services and take a skills-assessment inventory. Then, help your child outline a network of contacts, conduct informational interviews, and get help writing a resume to package those skills in a new way.

Parent Tip 90

Almost 36 percent of U.S. workers are employed in companies with fewer than 99 employees. Another 15 percent work for companies with 100–499 employees. This means that 51 percent of all U.S. jobs are with companies employing fewer than 500 workers.

For new college graduates, this means that many good jobs will be with smaller organizations that may not have large human resources departments to devote to recruiting and monitoring the Internet for applicants. Opportunities in these smaller companies are more likely to be identified through networking.

Jobs in smaller organizations often offer more opportunity at the price of a lower starting salary and fewer benefits. A young adult may have to trade a bigger salary and benefit package for the opportunity to get a foothold in a business or organization that is in its emerging or growth phase.

Industries have phases, including an emerging phase, a growth phase, a mature phase, and a declining phase. Many young adults will need to be more entrepreneurial in their thinking than their parents were. This is because large organizations in their mature and declining phases have been shedding employees by the thousands in recent years. Young people need to target companies on the rise. They need to be willing to pitch in and do whatever it takes to make the business grow. They also need to limit their student loan debt in college so they will be free to take advantage of growth opportunities once they are out of school.

Parent Tip 91

"Lifelong learning" does not mean "lifelong college classes" and "lifelong student loans."

Everyone, regardless of education level, will be required to be lifelong learners in the 21st century. Many jobs have yet to be created, and these jobs will require workers who have the basic transferable and specific-content skills to learn them. But this does not mean that everyone needs more degrees. Lifelong learning

(continued)

(continued)

means that all workers must be willing to learn new things, which they can do in both formal and informal ways.

Formal learning is offered in college and universities, technical and trade schools, apprenticeships, GED study programs, and classroom-based education an employer provides on site or makes available to employees online. If your employer sends you to in-house training to use the new human resources or billing software the company just purchased, this is formal training. If your employer asks you to take an accounting class online to help you on your job, this is formal training.

Informal learning takes place in many settings. Professional groups such as those in human resources, advertising, and organizational training and development often do informal instruction at monthly meetings. Many people have developed their public speaking skills by participating in a group such as Toastmasters. Conventions and conferences offer training opportunities for members of their organizations and industries. Many professional workers must take frequent non-credit continuing education courses to maintain their credentials. Other people develop skills in budgeting, project management, and marketing through participation in volunteer organizations and working for charitable causes. All of these are examples of lifelong learning that takes place outside a traditional classroom and doesn't drive the learner deeper into debt. All are "resume builders" that can help a person get ahead.

Ongoing learning and the advancement of individual knowledge will be the key to career success in the future. It no longer works to have an attitude of "That's not my job." Help your child understand that the jobs people will be doing in the next 20 years will be constantly changing. The ability to learn and re-learn new things will be the main factor in your child's' employability. But this lifelong learning may or may not require another college degree.

Parent Tip 92

Many young adults experience stress after college due to their debt-to-income ratio. This is the percentage of gross monthly income that must be used to pay student loans and credit card debt. Studies indicate that the higher the monthly student loan payment, the more difficult it is for young people to manage stressful feelings about total debt. In addition, the longer the student loan payment goes on, the more students are likely to feel burdened by their student loan debt.

Students who know how much they are borrowing as they borrow and who receive counseling about repayment at the time they leave school feel less burdened by their education debt after graduation. Make sure your child is an informed consumer of higher education debt. Starting as a freshman, your child should review financial aid awards with you each semester and calculate exactly how much he has borrowed and how much his payments will be after he leaves school.

Parent Tip 93

Student loans are based on the idea that with more education, an individual will have more skills, and those skills will help him earn more money to pay off the student loans.

This scenario assumes that life goes forward in a positive, upward direction; for example, the student gets a good job that is not vulnerable to layoffs and does not experience any life detours on the way to greater and greater income.

This has not been the experience of many young adults who took out student loans in recent years. Make sure that if your child is taking out student loans in his name, he keeps them to a minimum and knows how he will pay them back after graduation.

Parent Tip 94

A student considering graduate school needs to make a careful inventory of his existing student loans using the College Loan Worksheet in Chapter 8. The interest continues to accrue on unsubsidized federal loans and most federal consolidation loans while a student is in graduate school. The unpaid interest on undergraduate loans can significantly increase the overall debt the student faces once he is out of graduate school and paying back both undergraduate and graduate school loans.

Parent Tip 95

As the pool of traditional-age students age 18 to 25 decreases, colleges are increasingly marketing to young adults in their 20s and 30s. Internet pop-up boxes routinely tell these young people that they need a master's degree to get ahead or that they need to complete a bachelor's degree if they have not

(continued)

(continued)

already done so. The marketing message is "Buy more education or you will be left behind in the job market."

One figure rarely discussed is the amount of student loan debt carried by young adults who started college but never completed a degree. Already burdened by student loan debt from the past, these young adults are now a target market of colleges and universities.

If an employer pays the tuition costs, that's great. It is always good insurance to complete a degree if possible. But if a young person is paying out of pocket for a degree or planning to pay for it with student loans, he needs to research the job market before going back to school. This is true whether he is completing a bachelor's degree or starting a master's degree program.

The educational credential itself is only one side of the supply/demand equation when it comes to education and jobs. The demand for graduates with the credential is the other side of the coin. If there is no demand for an educational credential in a community or if there are already numerous people with that credential who are unemployed or underemployed, getting the credential may not help the young person get ahead.

A young adult considering going back to school needs to do his homework. He should be cautious about adding to his debt/income ratio by taking out more student loans. More training does not necessarily mean more academic degrees. More academic degrees does not necessarily mean more job opportunities.

Parent Tip 96

A new college graduate who doesn't have an initial career focus can benefit by writing a 30-second want ad. This is a brief one-paragraph description of the skills he enjoys using and the values that are important to him as they relate to employment.

Encourage your child to fill in the blanks as follows:

- These are the skills I most enjoy using:
- These are the values and priorities that are important to me:
- This is the kind of work environment I work best in:

Have your child summarize his responses in a paragraph, which he can then share with a variety of people in his network, asking each person, "What jobs does this sound like to you?"

Depending on the background of the person he is talking to, your child will identify different job titles in different industries that use similar skills and satisfy similar values. Having identified potential job titles, your child can conduct informational interviews with people working in those roles to find out the work experience and education needed to get hired. He can then redo his resume and reorganize his job search to target one of those positions.

CHAPTER 12

Summary

Every parent of a college student knows about the "five-year plan." This is a humorous way of saying that the average college student now takes four and a half to five years to complete what used to be a four-year degree.

Avoiding the Five-Year Plan

The easiest way to avoid the five-year plan is to use the ideas in this book to intervene in your child's life in a positive way. Here is a summary of the things you can do to help your child graduate from college in just four years.

1. Make sure your child is academically prepared for college (Chapter 9).

   This means insisting that your child take an academically rigorous curriculum in high school, one that includes four years of college-prep math. Even if your child decides to be a French major, she will have to pass college algebra to get a four-year degree. If she decides to go into a technical program after high school, she may need more math than college algebra. Opting out of math in high school will add time and money to your college costs. This is true whether your child plans to attend a four-year college or university, a community college, or a technical school.

2. Support your child in starting career exploration in high school (Chapters 4 and 5).

   The purpose of career exploration in high school is to help your child begin to connect education with careers. It is not to force your child to choose a career path prematurely. Basic career exploration in high school will expand your child's self-understanding. It will allow her to gather data upon which to make informed, rather than emotional, decisions about where to go to college and what subject to major in when she is there.

3. Encourage your child to take at least 15 credit hours a semester in college.

   Don't confuse the full-time requirements for financial aid and health insurance with the full-time academic requirements your child will need to complete college in four years.

   Financial aid and health insurance providers usually consider a student taking 12 credit hours a full-time student. Your child will need to take 15 credit hours a semester in order to complete a 120-credit-hour degree in eight semesters.

   A four-year college degree is made up of 120 to 130 college credit hours. If you divide 120 credit hours by eight semesters (fall and spring semesters, with summers off), you'll find that it will take at least 15 hours per semester for your child to graduate in four years. This assumes your child is settled on a major in time to complete her pre-major requirements sophomore year (Chapter 6) and is not required to take remedial courses (Chapter 9). It also assumes she does not drop or fail any of the classes she attempts.

4. Do not rely on your child taking a lot of college credit in high school to decrease the time it takes to get a college degree (Chapter 9).

   The length of time it takes for students to complete a degree does not necessarily decrease with college credit earned in high school. This is because there is no one-size-fits-all formula for making the most of college credit in high school.

   There are many variables that impact how college credit eventually applies toward a degree. Unless your child knows the college she will be attending and has identified a major, she cannot know for certain how the courses she has taken in high school will apply to her college degree. She can also inadvertently add pressure to her freshman year in college by jumping into sophomore-level coursework freshman year.

   If your child is eligible to take high school honors courses, encourage her to do so to ensure she is academically prepared for college.

But pay for college credit only if you are confident that those credits will apply to your child's degree and you are sure your child can handle jumping over freshman courses and starting in sophomore-level classes.

5. Don't normalize frequent college major changes (Chapter 6).

   It will be impossible for your child to graduate in four years if she waits until her junior year to select a major.

   Help your child separate choosing a major from choosing a first career. Show her how it will take both education (in the form of a degree) and work experience (in the form of paid and unpaid employment) to be marketable upon graduation. That work experience can include part-time jobs during the academic year, summer jobs, internships, and volunteer positions.

   For most jobs, the major is not the career. Shifting from major to major in the hopes of finding a career direction is a waste of time and money. Some majors have a direct relation to a job title; most do not.

   If your child is interested in a major that does not have a direct connection with a career, focus your energies on helping her get work experience while in college that will make her marketable once she has her degree.

6. Make sure your child works no more than 20 to 25 hours a week during the academic year.

   Your child will need at least two hours of outside study for every credit hour she is in class each semester. This means that the total time commitment for a first year college student taking 15 credit hours is 45 credit hours for school per week: 15 hours in class and 30 hours of study.

   Forty hours a week is a full-time job. A 15-credit-hour academic schedule is called a "full-time load" in college. Working 20 to 25 hours a week at a part-time job on top of this time commitment for study means that a total of 65 to 70 hours of your child's time is spoken for before any socializing is factored in. Help your child with the time-management challenges of working while in college before she leaves for school.

7. Talk about the consequences of "student swirl" before your child selects a college.

   "Student swirl" is the practice of changing colleges mid-degree.

This will invariably cost you and your child time and money. Some courses taken at the first college won't transfer or apply to the second, and your child will be behind other students at the second school in meeting prerequisites for certain majors.

Most high school students apply to several schools as part of the college-admissions process. Choosing a college that is too much of a "reach" in terms of distance away from home and loss of social connections with friends attending colleges closer to home can prompt some students to switch colleges at the end of freshman year. In doing so, they often leave generous financial aid packages behind them.

Don't let your child's choice of college be so much of a reach that your child doesn't want to stay at the institution. Talk about the financial consequences of changing colleges up front.

8. Don't be afraid to say no.

   Higher education is a multi-billion-dollar business. High school juniors and seniors are a major target market for this business. Part of the marketing strategy of colleges and universities is to convince your child that choosing the "right" college is a life-or death decision, a decision that is primarily hers alone.

   A college education is a huge commitment of family resources, including money, time, and emotion. If you feel your child will not be successful at a particular school or that your child will graduate with a level of student loan debt that will be difficult to repay, do not feel guilty standing firm against the marketing pressure.

   Keep the end in mind. Remember that there is a goal beyond getting into college. It is getting out of college and getting on with a happy, productive adult life.

9. Honor the red flags.

   If your child doesn't want to go to college, think about other options (see Chapter 10). Focus on her other strengths (see Chapter 5) and help her network (see Chapter 3) to find other opportunities. Consider a gap year (see Chapter 10) to help her recharge and refocus.

10. Be honest about your child's adaptive skills (Chapter 5).

    If your child lacks the basic adaptive skills she needs to live away from home, begin teaching and reinforcing those skills in high school. Set boundaries. Be clear about who will pay for failed, repeated, or dropped classes before your child leaves for college. Be clear about who is going to pay off any student loans.

11. Give yourself permission to get involved in your child's career planning.

    Offering your child support and connections is not the same thing as dictating your child's career choice. Career planning is about how education plays out in the job market. Because you are in the job market and have connections, you are a valuable resource in your child's career planning. Career services on campus are important, but they can only help your child so far. Encourage your child to use the services available on campus, but help her identify additional resources and employment opportunities as well.

    You are one of your child's best resources for career planning. Chances are you wouldn't tell a friend who was looking for work to move 500 miles away and figure it out on her own. Give your child the same support and encouragement you would give a friend. Don't be afraid to help your child in the positive ways outlined in this book.

Out of College and Into the Workforce

Here are some additional things you can do to make sure your child is successful once she is out of school.

1. Make sure your child understands networking (see Chapter 3).

   Networking means interacting with people to get and give career information. In the old economy, networking wasn't important. Employees who worked in the same job for the same company for 40 years didn't need to know how to network. In the new economy, workers face a much less stable situation. They will have a series of jobs with different employers with periods of unemployment in between. Knowing how to network to find work will be critical to long-term success. Your child must know what her skills are and how to communicate her skills to people she knows, as well as communicate them to people she doesn't know in situations such as a job interview.

   Your child will be entering a workplace that is in the midst of major structural and economic changes. New jobs are emerging and old jobs are going away. Your child will need to know what is going on. The most accurate and timely information about job opportunities will come from conversations with people currently employed in stable jobs and with people connected to emerging industries and organizations.

2. Keep the "big picture" in mind.

   Young people age 18–25 are not known for taking a long-term view of life. It is important for you, as the parent, to keep things in perspective. In addition to asking, "Where should my child go to college?" you should be asking, "How is my child going to support herself once she gets out of school?" If you keep the big picture in mind, you will be better able to advise your child on education and employment choices.

3. Make sure your child understands the importance of lifelong learning.

   People who want to move forward in the 21st century economy will need to be lifelong learners. They must constantly update their current skills and learn new ones. They must convey a can-do attitude and contribute more than the minimum to each organization for which they work. Make sure your child understands that although she has completed a degree or certificate, her education isn't over. It is just beginning.

4. Keep a positive attitude.

   With all the turbulence in today's economy, it is easy to let your adult fears take over and transmit them to your child. This is especially true if you have experienced financial fallout during a recession or lost a job as a result of global economic change.

   But your child is not mid-career; she is at the beginning of her career. Have confidence in her ability to get established and move ahead. There will always be opportunities for educated, energetic, hardworking young adults who have good communication skills and a willingness to learn. In helping your child with career planning, you are preparing her to succeed in an entry-level career. With the right foundation of education and work experience and with confidence in her skills and networking abilities, your child will have the tools she needs to find her way in uncertain times.

5. Finally, recognize when it is time to let go.

This book has given you practical tools and strategies to be an effective parent around career and education issues. It has taught you how to provide "just-in-time" information and resources at each step of your child's career and educational planning process without hovering along the way.

If you have read this book and tried to apply the things you learned in it, you have done your part. You have helped your child identify her options and articulate her skills. You have taught her how to network. You have offered your support.

Now it is time to park your helicopter in the hangar and let go. It is up to your child to decide where to fly from here.

Parent Tip 97

You can find more tips, updated information, and links at my blog: http://guidetocollegeandcareers.blogspot.com/.

APPENDIX

College-Related Acronyms

ACG	Academic Competitiveness Grant
ACT	American College Testing Program
AP	Advanced Placement
CLEP	College Level Examination Program
COA	Cost of Attendance
EFC	Expected Family Contribution
FAFSA	Free Application for Federal Student Aid
FAN	Financial Aid Notification (award letter)
FAO	Financial Aid Office
FAT	Financial Aid Transcript
FDSLP	Federal Direct Student Loan Program
FFELP	Federal Family Education Loan Program
FSEOG	Federal Supplemental Educational Opportunity Grant
FWS	Federal Work-Study
GPA	Grade Point Average
GSL	Guaranteed Student Loan (Stafford Loan)
IB	International Baccalaureate
ISIR	Institutional Student Information Report
NMSQT	National Merit Scholarship Qualifying Test

(continued)

(continued)

PC	Parent Contribution
PJ	Professional Judgment
PLUS	Parent Loans for Undergraduate Students
PSAT	Preliminary Scholastic Assessment Test
SAP	Satisfactory Academic Progress
SAR	Student Aid Report
SAT	Scholastic Assessment Test
SC	Student Contribution
SEOG	Supplemental Educational Opportunity Grant
SLMA	Student Loan Marketing Association (now Sallie Mae)
SLS	Supplemental Loan for Students
SMART	National Science and Mathematics Access to Retain Talent Grant
SSIG	State Student Incentive Grants
TEACH	Teacher Education Assistance for College and Higher Education Grant

Index

D

E

F

G

H

I

J–K

L

M

N

O

P

Q–R

S

T

U–V

W–Z